Stock Market Investing for Beginners:

Mastery of The Market with Confidence and Discipline

Strategies to Earn Passive Income, Grow your Wealth and Start Making Money Today. Day Trade for Living.

information contained within this document, including, but not limited to, — errors, omissions, or inaccuracies.

Table of Contents

Introduction

You might have probably heard of how good it is to invest in stocks. In fact, you might have even heard of how good this whole investment concept is. By putting in a considerable amount of money on something, you are bound to make that amount grow by each passing year until you get twice the amount you invested or more. At least, that's how an investment works in theory.

You might have even heard of how a lot of people became successful purely from investing in stocks at the stock market. With a few key investments here and there, they were able to earn from multiple sources within their investment portfolio. Perhaps with the right timing and knowledge, you too can turn a fistful of dollars into a 6-digit amount in your net worth or, better yet, in your bank account.

But here is the teeny tiny problem:

You know absolutely nothing about investing in stock.

That might be a problem because how are you supposed to succeed in any field if you don't have some level of experience in it? There are some key differences in the concept of investing which means success here is not as straightforward as earning a salary. In fact, investing has more similarities to gambling than with any other means of earning money.

However, here is the good news. Despite how intimidating the whole market could be, there is absolutely a way to be successful here even if it is your first time venturing into it. The stock market actually does not discriminate when it comes to who will make it big. Experienced or not and regardless of what stocks you invest in, everybody always has the same potential for success here.

So, how can an absolute beginner make their first successful steps in the stock market? In this book, Stock Market Investing for Beginners: Mastery of the Market with Confidence and Discipline, I will lay out a road map to your success. Investing in stocks is not exactly as complicated or glamorous as shows and movies make it out to be. There is an art and science to it. By taking advantage of what is available for you, you can eventually start making successes here and there.

To do that, you must first learn the basics. Now, the introduction to the market is always the intimidating part which is why it is necessary that you ease yourself in to the entire process. From learning what kind of investor you are, the types of stocks that you want to invest in, and how you could possibly earn from your investments, the basics will set up the foundation from which you can build on your successes in the stock market.

Once we get through the more basic concepts, we would now start going over buying stock. There are quite a lot of skills to learn here from research and speculating which stocks are about to go up in value a lot in the next few days. This is where the science part comes into play as you must learn how to become precise and methodical with your investments on a regular basis.

One other crucial aspect of investing in stocks is learning what not to do. Over the years, there are countless investors who made several mistakes that cut their stay in the market short. The best way to capitalize on these mistakes is to learn what they are, how you can perform them, and what you can do to prevent yourself from getting into such situations.

The risk will also be one other crucial aspect that you will learn over the course of this book. There is nothing certain in the world of investments. Things might take a turn for the worse in an instant due to factors that were beyond your control. By learning how to deal with risk, you could at least build on your successes without unnecessarily putting yourself in situations where you lost more money than you ought to gain.

Once you have made your first successful investment, the next thing to learn is how to build on your successes. In here, you will be taught how to carefully expand on your investment portfolio while dealing with new challenges that come from maintaining the momentum of your success. At the very least, this should make sure that your stay in the stock market does not become a short one.

Now, you will be asking yourself "Can I do all of this and be successful?". The answer is yes. In here, you will also get acquainted with several successful investors and learn how they themselves made it big tin their respective markets. With their perspective, you might be able to learn a few tricks for yourself and make your own path towards success.

All in all, this is but a bird's eye view of what you will learn as you go through each page of the book. Do not worry, all of this information is based on several years' worth of personal experience in the market and condensed in a manner that is easy to understand for the greenest of beginners.

Is investing in the stock market demanding? Maybe. Is it easy enough for beginners to understand and succeed in? Definitely yes. Again, all that is needed is for you to get the basics right, arm yourself with the right tools and knowledge, and make the right movements at the right time. The rest then, as they say, is up to sheer dumb luck.

If the very notion of reaping the financial rewards from a relatively high-stakes activity excites you, then let us dive first into the world of stock market investing.

Have fun!

Chapter I: Easing in on the Market

Picture this scene:

You are at home going through a news program. As soon as news about stocks come up, you suddenly switch to another channel. Why is this so?

There are quite a lot of reasons for this but the primary one is that you find the information being given to you a bit too intimidating. Those charts, graphs, numbers, and trends do sound important but they are presented in a manner that could scare off anyone who knows next to nothing about investments. It does not even help that they use industry-exclusive jargon which makes the segments even a bit more intimidating for non-investors.

Here is the thing, though: All that news about the stock market? They were meant for people who are already in it. So how can a beginner like you get an appreciation of the entire market?

To do that, there are a few basic concepts that you need to understand first.

(NOTE: The chapter will cover very basic stuff about stock investing. If you think you can get the gist of the chapter without reading it, you may proceed to chapter 2. But if not, I recommend that you go through this part first.)

What is Stock?

Let's get the most basic thing out of the way. What exactly is a stock? The definition of what constitutes stock can get rather complicated but the most basic concept of it is a claim of sorts on the assets and earnings of a company.

So how does stock exactly come into play? What you have to understand is that every corporation out there has a finite amount of capital to use in order to function properly. To get more capital, they need to ask for money in exchange for a portion of what that company owns and earns.

In essence, when you invest in stocks, you personally bind yourself to the existence, success, and overall longevity of a company. In short, you become a shareholder of that company. And when that company earns, you do.

Now, there will be a more extensive discussion on stock in the coming chapters. What you have to be concerned with now is that a stock always refers to a long-term relationship with a company. How you earn from your investments depends greatly on when you invested on a certain share and how that company from which that share came from performs on a regular basis.

What is the Stock Market?

The stock market is simply the place where stocks get issued, bought, traded, and sold either over a physical counter or through the various stock exchanges. Nearly every country has their own stock markets and dedicated stock exchange. Without these, the economy of that country tends to be rather stagnant or worse, non-functioning.

The purpose of any stock market is always two fold. The first is to **Provide Capital.** Now, as was stated a few paragraphs before, companies need capital in order to operate. And to get capital, they need investors. To get the attention of potential investors, they don't have to advertise over the radio or through print.

Instead, they get themselves publicly listed in the local stock market. Once they are listed, all of the stocks that they can trade will be publicly listed for trade. Once stocks are traded, capital comes pouring in to that company.

Here's an example: Let us say that Company A needs capital. As such, they get themselves listed in the local stock market where they issued 1 million shares for $5.00 each. Provided that all of these stocks are sold, the company gets 1 million shareholders each bringing in $5.00 per share to boost the company's capital by $5 million.

Of course, they could get the capital through loans but selling shares is one way of getting such amount without incurring debt and paying interest charges for such.

The second purpose is for investors to **Share Profit.** There are several ways on how you can profit from stock but they mostly come in two categories. The first is through passive means where the share earns in dividends for the investor over a period of time.

The second is through more active means by way of a trade. If, for example, the investor bought 6 shares at $10.00 each, he has the option to keep them under his name for as long as possible or sell them at a time when the same stocks for the same company are priced at $20.00 each. In essence, he got his initial investment back plus a 100% bonus. This helps the company gain more investors without releasing new shares while the investor gets to earn from each of their investments.

What You Need To Know About the Stock Market

As of now, the idea of jumping in to any stock market can be intimidating for you as a beginner. Just to make sure that your entry into the market goes as smoothly as possible, here are a few more things that you need to know about the stock market.

1. Market Indexes

When you watch stock market news, you might have noticed those little figures that go up and down. These are basically what are called market indexes which tells you how a certain class of stock or company is performing under the current market environment. Some news channels would use data from the S&P 500 or the Dow Jones Industrial Average to tell you the performance of one type of stock, corporation, or even an entire sector of the market.

A market index becomes important as it tells you, as an investor, on how to proceed in the next few days. Should you dump your shares and sell them cheap? Should you purchase new stocks on a certain company? Should you keep holding on to those stocks in the hopes that their prices go up in a few months or so? Your market index will tell you exactly that.

2. Stock Trading

A good investor knows to either diversify their portfolio or hold on to some stock index funds. These are actually legitimate strategies to sustain oneself in any market. However, if you are craving a bit more action, then you should consider trading stocks. If you time your trades right, you can earn quite a lot from your investments even if you just started with a fistful of dollars.

Stock traders are often classified by the frequency of their activity. There are those day traders who, simply put, trade stocks every day. There are also periodic traders who regularly make huge trades every few months or so. There are traders who do their activities exclusively on the physical stock exchanges and then there are those that do theirs online.

You will get to learn more of stock trading as you go through this book. What you have to understand now is that this activity will require a lot of research more than any other stock related activity. Tools, charts, and every other asset out there that can help you monitor and predict where stocks rise and fall can help you in this aspect.

3. **Bull or Bear?**

Do keep in mind that venturing into any stock market comes with a certain set of risks. It's up to you to pay attention of these risks in order to survive.

How would you know, then, that it is okay to venture into a certain sector of the stock market now? There are quite a lot of terms that seasoned investors but most use "bull" or "bear".

A bull market is simply a market where conditions are most favorable to investors. You will notice that you are in a bull market when the investors are quite confident in their transactions. Think of it like a poker table where the dealer shows his hand a lot. The players are getting cocky with their bets because they know what comes next and they can prepare accordingly.

A bear market, on the other hand, is where the prices for stocks are nearing free-fall. The threshold varies from market to market but you can be certain that investors here are either being more cautious with their transactions or, if worse comes to worst, start pulling out of the area.

As a beginner, you should know which economic pattern is present in your market so you would know how to take advantage of the situation. Your only solace is that markets tend to last longer as bulls instead of bears. If you find yourself dealing in a bear market, you can be certain that the downturn will not last for long.

4. Crashes vs. Corrections

Crashes and corrections are basically drops in the overall stock market. Where they differ is the percentage of the drop. When the drop is no more than 10%, that's a correction. But if the drop was sudden as symbolized by a downward spike in the trend, then this is a crash.

Crashes often tell you that the market is turning bear. But do remember that this downturn does not last long. Stock markets tend to rise up in value over time.

What you have to understand is that crashes and corrections happen more often than you think. Thus, discipline is necessary on your part to last long in the market. Long-term planning and careful allocation of resources should help you survive through a crash.

There are even tools out there that can help you determine how long you can recover from any sudden downturn. And you will learn of these a few chapters later.

5. **Diversification**

Although you cannot avoid downturns in the market, what you can control is your investment portfolio. A mistake beginner's make is failing to diversify on their investments. This means sticking to the stocks that they are the most comfortable with without venturing into other types.

This is rather precarious as you fail to provide a safety net of sorts on your investment. For example, if you invest solely on one sector, what happens to you when that sector drops? All of your investments would drop as well along with the overall value of your portfolio.

Believe it or not, a lot of things that are beyond your control can change the very outlook in a certain market. This could range from massive political upheavals, problems in economics and regulations, and even the outbreak of diseases.

Risk management is a key skill that you must develop when venturing into any stock market. You have to know which investments that you are bound to make carry the biggest risks and determine whether or not such risks can affect your overall portfolio.

Also, patience is required as building a portfolio takes a while. You can even look into mutual funds and index funds to instantly diversify your portfolio. There are other strategies that you can use to diversify your portfolio and, like always, you will get to know of them later on.

To Conclude

Is it intimidating to start out in the stock market?

Technically, it shouldn't be but that does not stop people from actually avoiding the market in its entirety. Some think that the market is too ruthless that anyone who is just starting might end up getting overwhelmed. Some are just too afraid of making bad investments that they end up not making any in the first place.

The truth is that, indeed, the stock markets are rather demanding. They are not that lenient to the point that you could be rewarded for a bad investment. However, they are not that completely ruthless that only those who have made it big can continue on earning here.

The point is that everyone has the same chances of success regardless of their experience in the market. Everyone can take advantage of the same opportunities and suffer from the same downturns. It is all a matter of being mindful of the current condition of the market and playing to your strengths accordingly.

Now, if that apprehension with the market is gone, it is time to get into the basics of buying your first stocks.

Chapter II: Investments

What are investments exactly? They are basically items that you put money in with the consideration that such thing would make that money grow for you. What makes investment different from gambling is that you are expected to know what you are exactly putting your money in and how it's going to make a profit for you unlike a wager.

But when we ask the WHAT when it comes to investments, what we are trying to ask is "in what form do they come in?". As such, getting acquainted with the stuff that you are about to buy and trade in the stock market and how you will eventually interact with them is rather crucial for any investor.

Stocks and The Stock Market

As was mentioned a few chapters ago, the stock market is a place where you can buy, sell, and trade all kinds of investments. As such, there are quite a number of ways to make money here.

But what exactly is the market's primary commodity? That comes in the form of, well, stocks. As was mentioned, stocks are proof of your ownership over a company's assets and income in exchange for providing for the company's capital.

What makes stocks so great as investment options is that their profitability is directly affected by the overall performance of a company. If the company does well, its value grows. And when the value of the company grows, so does the value of your share.

And this is where you can profit from your stocks by either trading your ownership of your stock to another according to the current value. If you bought stocks for cheap and that company's value grew by several digits in the market, you could effectively earn more than 200% of your initial investment through trading under the right conditions.

But if you do choose to hold over your ownership of the stocks, you can still profit from it. A company has the option of distributing a portion of its profits to the shareholders. As such, it is important that you read the fine print on the stocks specifically on what benefits you could reap from being a shareholder to the company before you agree to invest in that entity.

The point here is that stocks are generally viable options for first-time beginners. A lot of investors who succeeded out there have focused solely on stocks and made a lot of money before retiring like Warren Buffet. Of course, the potential for success in that stock is going to be dependent on that company.

This is why it is important that you can track and predict where a company is going performance-wise. For instance, if you feel that the company is failing, you may trade your stocks before the prices drop. This way, you can bail out on the company with a sizeable portion of your investments intact.

The Types of Stock

When we talk about stocks, we often think that they come in mostly the same form. However, the truth is that stocks usually come in two form. They are:

A. **Common**

When people talk about stocks in general, they most likely are talking about this type. As the name implies, common stocks are, well, common. They are publicly traded in stock markets and represent your claim of ownership over a portion of the company and its dividends. In short, most of the stocks you will find in the stock market fall under this category.

One neat feature with stocks is that they yield high returns as the years pass by way of a growing capital. In short, if a company performs well, the prices of their stock increases. This does not matter if those stocks have yet to be sold or currently in the ownership of an investor. All stocks will get a price increase so as long as the company performs well.

Of course, that works the other way around. If a company performs poorly or is in the verge of bankruptcy, the stocks become worthless. No matter the price you initially paid for them, those stocks will not be earning money for you.

B, Preferred

A preferred stock still offers the same benefits as common stocks in the sense that you get to own a portion of the company as well as a claim on its dividends. However, it is more limited in the sense that it does not give you the same voting rights as common stocks. In short, if you want to have a say on how the company is being managed, a preferred stock will not give you that right.

What it does offer instead is a fixed dividend. Unlike in common stocks where the value of the dividend can change according to the performance of a company, the dividends of a preferred stockholder will remain the same from the start to onwards. Usually, that dividend is several margins higher than what a common stock could offer.

One other benefit is that you will always get paid off first before common stockolders in case the company gets liquidated. However, just do keep in mind that creditors have to be paid off first before you.

Lastly, preferred stocks are callable. If, for some reason, the company wants to gain ownership of its stocks again, they can purchase your stocks for a premium.

At a glance, you can see that preferred stocks work more like bond than an actual share. It's something in between. But just to make things simple, preferred stocks are different in the sense that they allow you greater dividend sharing and the ability to get paid off first before the company closes.

Voting Rights and Stock Classes

Can a company make their own class of stocks? In a sense, yes. Although stocks are either common or preferred, companies have found ways to customize their stocks to come up with unique classes. Why would companies do this? Wouldn't they trade ownership of a portion of a company to complete strangers either way?

The truth is that ownership counts for not much when it comes to corporations. What matters more is voting rights. As the preferred stock has shown you, ownership really does not matter as much as having the right to determine how a company should be handled.

As such, companies are finding ways to get the capital from investors while retaining voting power to a select and often undisclosed group. As such, the different classes would often pertain to the different degrees of voting power being offered,

Here's an example, company XYZ would hold several shares to a select group with each share giving the holder ten votes. The other shares might just offer the standard 1 vote. So, if there are 100 shareholders split evenly within the two groups, that means that one group holds 500 votes while the other half holds only 50. Remember, majorities in companies are determined by the total number of votes owned, not the number of shareholders.

What are Stock Options?

Options are basically another form of stock with a more fluid pricing model. When you buy an option, you are technically close to gambling as the price of that stock could go up and down depending on how the company performs for that period.

Sounds risky, right? Not exactly. When you buy an option instead of the standard individual stock, you give yourself a stronger buying power over those stocks over a limited period of time. In other words, you have the option to either buy or sell that stock within a set period of time. Better yet is that you don't have to own the option in order to sell or trade them.

Of course, that fluctuating price could be rather risky. There is a change that the prices could drop severely for several periods. This means that you might be incurring losses for over a period of time depending on the performance of the company.

As such, stock options are great if you are aiming for a high-stakes, high-reward strategy in your investments. However, that also makes them risky for the uninitiated. Master the basics of the other stocks and investments first before you consider adding options to your investment portfolio.

The Other Kinds of Investment

Let's get this out of the way: in the stock market, there is no need to physically get a hold of the stocks and assets that you will buy and trade. In fact, what you are going to transact with over and over here will be documents signifying your ownership of such items.

That would make for a rather safe platform to do business in as there is no risk of the actual physical item being degraded or damaged through every transaction. In fact, depending on the nature of the stock, these items would not even move from where they are currently deposited. Their ownership only changes hands from one person to another.

Also, risk is directly affected by the nature of the stock itself. Of course, risk is directly proportional to the reward. There are stocks that are always good options to invest in regardless of the economy and then there are those that yield the best possible rewards but tend to be riskier depending on the situation. A good investor will know which stocks to invest in to balance the rewards with the risks.

With that out of the way, it is time to get to know which kinds of stocks you may want to invest in the market.

A. Cash and Commodity

At the bottom most portion of the risk ladder are cash and commodities. They are considered to be the lifeblood of any stock market as the frequency of trading activity regarding these stocks will often directly affect the performance of the economy. And even if the economy takes a turn for the worse, these stocks often remain viable investment options and could prove to be an effective safety net for your investment portfolio.

The only problem with this type of commodity is their comparatively low reward. Since they offer the least risk, their margin for profit growth for the investor is relatively low.

Gold

This metal is perhaps one of the oldest stock options to date. In fact, people have been trading gold for various commodities since way before the Egyptians built their pyramids. What makes Gold a safe first-time investment is its appeal. However, do keep in mind that much of this appeal is anchored on scarcity and fear. As such, the price of gold tends to fluctuate depending on factors beyond your control.

If you choose to invest in gold, you have to be mindful of the fact that your only protection against a price drop for this commodity is based on external factors. In fact, the price of gold tends to fluctuate a lot. Your only solace for this commodity is that never has the price of gold drop below the negatives.

An understanding of scarcity is also necessary to make the most out of gold. In essence, prices of gold rise up when scarcity and fear are quite high. Thus, if you are the person that would want to secure your finances in case something goes terribly wrong across the world, gold might be a good investment option for you.

Cash Deposits and other Bank Products

As the name imply, these investments are offered by banks. Bank products usually involve savings accounts and money market accounts. A cash deposit, on the other hand, is simply a loan that you give to the bank with the consideration that such amount will be returned to you with interest.

Like gold, bank products are still low-risk investments. In fact, you could expect no more than 2% for returns every year with these type of investments. If you know how inflation works, you would know that 2% will not be enough for profit out of these investments.

In essence, they are are safe options but are not great when you intend to make your money grow considerably over a period of time.

Cryptocurrencies

A newer form of investment, cryptocurrencies are unregulated digital investment options and are usually issued outside of the stock market. You may have heard one of these currencies,

Bitcoin, which has been gaining a lot of traction in recent years.

However, since they are relatively new and contain too many unknowns, it is best that you stay away from these investment options. In fact, there are many governments considering regulating these currencies due to a rise of many scams that involve them. As such, it would be still quite a while before Bitcoin and its ilk would get widespread market acceptance.

So as long as stock exchanges do not recognize these investment options, hold off on cryptocurrencies as of now.

B. Bonds and Securities

Another form of low-risk investments, these options are usually offered by institutions like the government and your typical private company.

Government and Corporate Bonds

Bonds are basically like cash deposits except that they are not issued by banks. When you purchase a bond from the government or a private corporation, you are essentially loaning that entity with your money with the expectation that they will return the same to you some time later with interest.

Bonds are generally safe for the sheer fact that the only time that you are not going to get your money back is if the one issuing the bond, for some reason, defaults. With government savings bonds, that is not likely to happen.

As for corporate bonds, however, they are riskier as the chances of defaulting are higher with a private company. Also, unlike your typical stock or share, a bond does not confer to you ownership over a portion of the company's assets and income.

What you have to understand is that both corporate and government bonds can give you as much as 3% of a return of your money over several years. This would mean that if you were to take your money out of the bond, you might risk decreasing your buying power. After all, the 3% growth rate is not keeping up with inflation.

Mortgage-based Securities

A security is, again, like a loan. However, this time, that loan is going to come with some real estate mortgages.

What makes securities different from bonds also is the way that you can earn profit here. Unlike a bond where the payout only occurs after the expiration of the term, mortgage-based securities can pay to an investor their interest on a monthly basis.

However, what makes these securities intimidating is their complexity. There are too many factors to consider when you determine your regular payout. Also, the risks tend to be higher depending on the terms of the mortgage.

As such, this investment option should only be considered by investors if they already have considerable experience in the market. First-time beginners like yourself should try out the low-risk, easier-to-understand investment options first.

C. **Investment Funds**

An investment fund is basically a conglomerate of money which came from different investors which would then be used for different products which include but are not limited to stocks, bonds, and other trade-able assets. What makes funds great is that they are the best indicator of a market's performance since they track the market index.

Mutual Funds

This investment option is basically a proxy investment. It will be operated by an agent authorized by you who will invest your money in your behalf and find ways to make such profit.

What makes mutual funds safe is that it's very own concept allows for instant diversification. The way you get your benefits from these, then, is either through the interest that they generate or when you sell your funds if the prices for such go up in the market.

The only downside in this option is that you will spend more in keeping them functional. As a matter of fact, a portion of your money would go about paying the services of your manager as well as the agents that they might employ in order to investments running.

As such, do consider this investment option as a mid-tier option. Start with the other low-risk investments first so that you could learn how to invest your own money for yourself. Once you are confident with your skills, you can then use mutual funds to quickly diversify your portfolio.

Index Funds

Like mutual funds, this fund will help you diversify in your investments quickly. The only difference with them is that index funds are managed passively. This means that you would have to deal with fewer fees which then leads to you keeping more of the returns you will make out of your investment.

However, that amount you will get in returns is directly proportional to the market index. If the index is low, your returns will be low. And vice versa.

If you are the investor who wants to put money on something and then not think too much about it, then this investment option might be ideal for you.

Exchange-Traded Funds

An ETF will function similarly to other funds. What makes it different is that it is one of the only funds that can be purchased directly from the stock market. This gives you even more control over how much you are going to pay for them and you will have to pay fewer fees to maintain them.

But, of course, the fund's profitability is directly tied to the performance of the market index. This can be circumvented to a degree if the fund tracks a broader index like what the S&P 500 has to offer.
As such, for beginning investors, this is a relatively safe fund to invest in.

D. Retirement and Other Savings Options

These investment options come in the form of accounts issued by banks and other financial institutions. Since their purposes and duration vary from one product to another, the risk and reward for retirement options can vary. Beginning investors like yourself can consider these options early on but great care and research must be done first before you start investing on them.

Also, it goes without mentioning that the maturity periods for these investment options are notoriously long. Only include them in your investment plan if you are into long-term planning and a whole lot of patience.

Lastly, these are not purely investment options per se. Rather, your retirement plans can be a tool for which you can venture into other investment options. The only requirement is that you have access to the funds stashed in these plans which means that they must have already matures if you want to make full use of them.

401K

A 401K is basically a retirement plan offered by a company mandated by the US Government. What can draw you to such an investment option is that, in here, the employer can offer something that could match what you have already invested in or, at least, a portion of it.

This matching feature is what makes a 401K rather beneficial if you want to play it safe as an investor. However, 401Ks function like your typical Mutual Fund without diversification. This means that the funds are in the hands of a manager that you have to constantly pay for their services.

Of course, a 401K is only available if you yourself are currently employed. The company that you currently work in is the only entity that can offer you such. Thus, your 401K options are rather limited in one lifetime.

IRA

Known properly as an Individual Retirement Account, IRAs are either tax-deferred or tax-free. This means that a portion of the money you invested won't be taken out just to fill up the government's coffers.

Also, an IRA gives you better control on what you can invest with it compared to a 401K. If you want, you can use the money to invest on other products like stocks, investments, and mutual funds if you like.

In short, IRA is a good option if you want reduce the risks, exert more control over your funds, and quickly diversify on your folio. Your key to success here will most definitely involve maxing out on your plan as soon as humanly possible.

Annuities

An annuity functions more like a contract between you and a financial institution usually an insurance company. Here, you pay something in bulk to the insurance company with the consideration of getting payed regularly by the company. It's kind of like a salary if you are already retired in the sense that you get it on a regular basis.

The good thing about annuities is that there is absolutely no risk involved with them. The only problem? There is no reward with them either. It's a good way to get a steady source of income if you are retired but there is no room for growth here.

As such, they are not the most ideal option for any investor. Nor should you even consider them as a jumping off point for other investment options.

E. Real Estate

Whether it involves buying buildings, renovating them, or selling, real estate is one of the most rewarding investment options out there. But that high reward often comes with a laundry list of risks and expenses. There are some methods you can use to mitigate your risks here but it does not remove the fact that real estate is a high-stakes investment route.

Beginners should not take on this option right away until they master the basics of the other forms of investment. Also, having a sizeable capital is needed for your activities here.

Property

Whether for commercial or residential purposes, it is hard to find a building right now that is priced less then a $50,000.00 for the entire structure excluding repairs. This might give the idea that those with little to no capital cannot engage in this investment route but crowd funding has been a rather viable funding option for investors here. The only downside is that you will have to share the profits with others, depending on the terms you agreed with them.
What makes this investment option also hard is in finding the right safety margin. The safety margin simply means the difference between your initial expenses incurred in buying and flipping the property and your asking price for the same based on the building;s current Fair Market Value.

You can't have the margin too wide or people might not buy the property. You can't also have the margin too narrow or you'd end up with a loss. Finding that sweet spot between expenses and the price will help you earn considerably from your building.

Of course, buying low and selling high isn't the only means to make money from your building. You can also rent the property for tenants to use which ensures a steady stream of income from your investments on a long-term basis.

Investment Trusts

This investment option works similarly to that of a mutual fund. This is because it takes the funds of several investors and then puts them into several income-generating projects. Also, Investment Trusts can be sold and traded in the stock market which makes them the cheaper property-based investment option that you can resort to.

Since you don't have to buy, renovate, and sell property, an investment trust is one of the best property-based options that a beginner can take advantage of. You might not earn a lot compared to selling actual properties but the income you will get will be dependable enough over a considerable period of time.

What NOT to Invest In

Now, the investments above only cover a fraction of what is actually available to you in the stock market and beyond. Although cryptocurrencies and annuities are not recommended, they can still be viable if you know what you are doing or, at the very least, have a sizable safety net to fall back on if things get worse.

However, there are those investment options that you should avoid investing now. These investments are either bad because of current market conditions or are just bad investments by their nature.. As such, here are some of the options that you should never even consider as a first time investor.

1. Subprime Mortgages

If investment options are buildings, then a subprime mortgage is that seedy club at the farthest end of a red light district. In essence, these mortgages are meant for the least trustworthy of creditors who are most likely to default on a loan. To invest on one is to ensure that you are not going to see a single penny out of the money you just loaned to someone else.

2. Penny Stocks

Usually, companies offer their stocks for no less than $5.00 which is pretty cheap. But there are companies that go cheaper and Wall Street folk call these stocks they offer as "penny stocks". Mostly, they can go as low as $1.00 or 50 cents which can sound appealing for new investors. Also, due to their low figures, the smallest of changes in their price can translate to massive changes in your gains.

But what makes them deadly is their deceptiveness. A penny stock is usually a tell-tale sign that that company is going bankrupt. It's one way for deceptive companies to dump on their stocks and leave the stock market with a sizeable portion of money.

Basically, they are the fronts of many pump and dump schemes which will leave investors with a dud stock in the long run.

3. Junk Bonds

They are alternatively known as high-yield bonds today because, technically speaking, a high yield of reward often connotes high risk. Junk bonds can be enticing to investors especially in a market with low interest rates.

But like penny stocks, a junk bond is often a sign that the company is going bankrupt or will go into default. If you own a junk bond from a company, you are mostly going to lose that investment, hence the term.

You can mitigate the risks by choosing a bond by way of a mutual fund but this does not remove the problem entirely. If you do not have all the information about that company or do not know how to speculate on their performance, don't take any bond from them just to be safe.

4. Private Placements

A private placement is simply a stock that was not publicly traded in the stock exchange. Right from the start, they are a turn-off as you must become an accredited investor first before you can even start investing on them. And how do you become accredited? It's either you have an income of $100,000.00 per year or have a net worth over $1 million.

But what makes private placements risky by themselves is that they are often used by deceptive promoters, assuring you with a lot of upsides without telling you of the potential risks. In essence, you will be investing on something that you do not have full information of which is close to gambling.

5. The Double Digit Return

There are those stocks that are just too good to be true. If you have ever heard of an investment that promises more than 10% returns per year, you should be careful. This will be the first thing being promoted to you followed by usual malarkey like "it's government backed!" or "it's insured!" and the oh-so-common "it's the next (insert famous company here)!".

You have to remember that no investment option out there would promise any return. Yes, some are insured and some do get backed by the government but no stock out there will ever promise you returns by the double digits. In fact, the best companies out there rarely offer 10% returns. Some are generous enough at 5% and some do offer the usual 2-3%. Nothing more.

Just keep this rule in mind: if the offer is too good to be true, it is.

To Conclude

So which investment option should you go first? That really depends on you. But if you are the one to want to keep your momentum in this market strong, it is best that you build a strong base.

To do that, it is best that you start with stocks and then diversifying your portfolio with other investment options later on. It's a good way of getting the feel of the market without overspending. At the same time, it is easy for you to bail out in case something goes wrong.

In short, start with stocks first and then venture into other investments later.

Chapter III: The Investor

As was previously stated, the stock market has plenty of opportunities for a person to earn from their stay there. But you might be wondering to yourself just how could you make a name for yourself as a stock market investor.

To answer that question, you have to determine what kind of role you want to play in the market. Understanding this role is crucial for determining your path towards success in the stock market. For this chapter, we would discuss on what major goal you may want to achieve in the market and the tools that you will need in order to make a name for yourself there.

What Kind of Investor are You?

Buying stocks at the market is very basic skill. However, each person buying and trading stock does so for different reasons. The role that you will play as an investor depends greatly on the level of risk you want to regularly deal with, the amount of research that you can and want to do for each investment, how much you know or can speculate as to where the overall economy is heading to, and the length of your intended stay in the market.

Sounds a bit confusing, right? To simplify things, investors always come in three forms which are as follows:

Active Investors

An active investor is perhaps one of the busiest yet more cautious people in the stock market right now. They do everything in their power to stay in the know when it comes to market trends, keep up with the latest news, and spend hours of research on every viable stock option before they start investing.

Buying and selling is not exactly their primary goal here. They pay attention to trends in the market and form their decisions based on those trends. They might not hold investments in the long term but they do take care to make sure that each investment they make counts.

Passive Investors

Where other investors aim for the biggest possible rewards from each investment they make, the passive investor aims for more reasonable gains and a generally stress-free stay in the market. These investors do not care if they have to pay more from each investment as long as they enjoy their stay in the market.

As such, passive investors often go for mutual funds as this allows for quick diversification of their portfolios while others do the dirty work for them. They do not gamble their money on up and coming companies but stick with what has already been established as successful.

Their overall goal here is to coast through the market as easily as possible. If the value of their stocks rise by at least 20% of what they initially purchased it, they might start selling them. It does not matter if a better price is out there. What matters for the passive investor is to make things as easy for them as possible.

The Speculator

There is earning money in the stock market and then there is earning money *fast*. Like the active investor, speculators also do their research but focus on stocks that are about to go up a lot in pricing because of some impending change. Perhaps a merger is about to happen between two companies which can boost prices for their stocks.

Once they know what stocks are about to go up, they would then buy these stocks before the change happens. And when prices go up, they would then sell the stocks according to the new price tag. They then repeat this process over and over again..

Speculators have the highest frequency in trading activities among all other investor types. This also means that they don't hold certain investments for long, selling what they have at the first opportunity of a price change.

The Bargain Hunter

Unlike other investors that focus on buying cheap and selling high, the bargain hunter finds stocks that are really cheap and hold them. They are not essentially aiming for huge, instant profit but long-term growth especially if a floundering company still shows promise of bouncing back.

Their tactics might go against what we have covered a chapter ago but many companies that managed to regain traction in the stock market owe their survival to bargain hunting investors. KMart, for example, suffered through times so bad that they were effectively taken of Wall Street. However, they managed to make it out of their predicament with the investments from bargain hunters.

To be a bargain hunter is to play the game like you are gambling. There is absolutely no assurance that a failing company is going to rise again. But if it does, the rewards that a bargain hunter could receive are comparatively large.

The Retiring Investor

These investors are in the market for the long-term and they do change tactics once they get older. For example, an investor of this type would be quite aggressive at a young age, buying high-risk stocks. As they grow older, they mellow down and start moderating their risks.

Once they reach retirement age, this investor would now focus on dividend stocks that will make them money in lieu of a monthly salary. This investor owes their survival to an ability to manage their risks smartly. They focus on quickly increasing the value of their investments at a young age and then switch to making such investments sustainable as they get older.

The Player

This investor has more qualities to share with a gambler than any other investor role out there. They understand that chaos and uncertainty is always present in any market and thus try to take advantage of such.

Regardless of how they get their funding, the player aims to increase their money in the fastest time possible. Whenever a new company enters into the market or massive changes are implemented, the player would be at the very front trying to take advantage of the frenzy that is generated. Once they are confident with the value, they will then cash out before the market stabilizes.

It's a rather high-risk strategy but players tend to receive the largest rewards relative to the risks they take. By timing your investments right, you might just be able to take advantage of sudden opportunities without losing a lot of money.

What Kind of Trader Are You?

Trading is a wholly separate process from investing. In fact, it's requirements as well as the dynamics here can be quite different from investing.

As such, it is best that you know what kinds of traders tend to flourish in the market right now.

The Scalper

Although that word comes with some serious negative connotations now, scalpers in the stock market are simply those traders who are in it to fulfill short-term goals. Their turnaround time is shorter than that of day traders and they tend to stick to very specific niches in the market.

Scalpers do not necessarily need a lot of capital due to how quickly they can move from one stock to another. However, they will need to have a steady flow of cash ready at the side in order to take advantage of sudden changes in the market.

Since their capital size is small, their target profit is also comparatively small. In fact, they focus on small gains more which, in due time, would accumulate to a substantial amount. To make scalpers easier to understand, think of them as those bargain shop owners. They sell things cheap, mostly at a loss per individual item, but tend to clear up their inventories on a faster rate.

The Day Trader

One step above scalpers, day traders also focus on short-term trades but their turnaround time is comparatively longer. In fact, they often aim for short, 20-minute trades which is why they can do multiple trades per day (hence the name).

Like scalpers, day traders do not have a sizeable capital. This is why they trade often so they can soften the blow of losses on a daily basis. In theory, the frequent activity and the small capital base will allow for a day trader to survive under tough conditions or bail out without having to part with what used to be valuable investments.

Due to their frequent activity, a day trader does not leave a position open for too long. As such, their potential for profit is rather limited. Again, they can be like scalpers in the sense that their victory conditions can be expressed in terms of volume-based value instead of per-item value.

The Swing Trader

A swing trader tends to hold on their trades for longer periods of time. Patience and a bit of faith is required with these traders as they do not have the time nor the resources to constantly monitor their trades.

By the name itself, you can determine that a swing trader will hold on to their trades until times get better. A "swing" in the market, if you will. Thus, they require a lot of capital in order to keep their investments going under tought financial conditions.

A benefit of holding off on frequent trading is that it allows a trader wider profit margins when they do open their investments for trade. Again, this is dependent on timing. When things start to go up, you can expect a swing trader to be the first to open for trading and reap maximum benefits.

The Position Trader

These traders are the very definition of "long term". Like swing traders, they can hold off on trading but for a ridiculously long period of time. In fact, it is not uncommon for a position trader to open a stock up for trader years after purchasing it. As such, they tend to not frequent the stock market a lot.

Holding off on a stock is rather challenging as it's value can go up and down depending on market conditions. As such, a huge capital is needed in order for a position trader to survive with their chosen strategy.

But all that patience does pay off in time. Under the right conditions, the potential payoff for position traders are massive. This could be chalked up to long-term planning or the ability to accurately predict what trend that stock will follow in the years to come but a position trader is in the best position (pun intended) to earn thousands for each stock that they trade.

The Main Takeaway:

These different investor and trader personalities are just indicating that everyone has a place in the market. Though there will be winners and losers in every period, it does not remove the fact that everyone has a chance to make it big in the market.

What is essential is that you pick a style that you are most comfortable with or, better yet, confident with. In short, you must play to your strengths in order to make it big in the stock market. That is provided, of course, that you know what your strengths are.

Chapter IV: The Investor's Arsenal

What separates a good investor from the rest? If the firs thing that comes to your mind is "experience", you are basically half right. But, since we stand on the theory that you don't need experience to achieve your first-time success in the stock market, we can take that factor out of the equation.

What do we have left, then? That would the tools, skills, and even qualities that you must possess as a stock investor. As such, here are some of the things that you need in order to make your stint as a stock investor a rather successful one.

A. Essential Skills and Qualities

Let's start with the things that are innate to you or, at the very least, you will have to develop for yourself. Looking the part of an investor is just the start so that three-piece suit and capital will be where your baseline. From that point, you can start acquiring the essential characteristics of a stock investor which are as follows:

1. Analysis

A stock market investor is going to do a lot of analysis in order to remain competitive in the market. This is rather crucial as the stock market is rather dependent on trends and other outside economic factors.

A more practical explanation for the need of stock market analysis is that it allows you to determine what approaches, strategies, and tools are needed to respond to a trend in market. Later on in the book, you will learn the core characteristics of different market environments and how they are best responded to in order to survive. By using analysis, you will learn how to adjust your strategies while the market is approaching that certain condition.

The point here is that a good investor knows to find a balance between making the right amount of money and taking the right action at the right time. The former is for profit and the latter for survivability. Your analytical skill will help you meet these two different goals at the same time.

2. Research

What separates investing from gambling is that the former demands that you do not go in blind. You have to be armed with all the information that you could possibly gather before you place your bets on something.

When you encounter possible stocks in the market, you should resist all urge to invest on it ASAP. You have to take the time to learn everything about you can about that company, what trends would affect the performance of that sector, and even who runs that company before you start buying and trading stocks.

And how exhaustive is research in stock market investing? You will have to keep track of whatever economic changes, political movements, and inter corporate announcements to make sure that you are investing on the right stock.

In fact, you must develop a preference for reading through charts and tables to keep track of how stocks are performing. This is also quite crucial in downturns as a well-informed investor can take advantage of such and make a profit where others are losing money. At the very least, the right amount of information will help you make better-informed decisions.

3. Calm

Remaining calm is a crucial yet oft-overlooked quality in stock investors. A common mistake beginners make is to panic when they are at a loss. Thus, you get all those pictures of distressed stock investors gnashing and pulling their hair at the Stock Exchange during the economic crisis of the 2000s.

Do not get the wrong idea. There is actually no way out there to fully avoid stress in high-stakes environments like the Stock Market. However, getting overwhelmed by your stress tends to make you do some stupid mistakes which makes things worst for you.

There have too many instances in the past when panicking investors dump all their stocks at the first sight of a downturn, not realizing that the entire problem could have been solved without them incurring losses. A calm investor, on the other hand, carefully adjusts their strategy in order to take advantage of the sudden change of plans.

4. Records Management

A stock investor must also keep a record of every transaction they have ever made. This will serve two purposes. First is for archiving as a record will help you keep track of all investments you have made and how they are faring currently.

The second reason is more personal. By keeping documents, you can at least track your progress as an investor. Are your strategies doing well? What sectors have you yet to venture into? Is it time to call it quits? Your records will tell you that and more.

5. Discipline

I've gone on many times on the difference between investing and gambling because a lot of investors treat the former as if it were the latter. In fact, many go to the stock market thinking that it's just some fancier casino minus the slot machines.

Your overall goal as a stock market investor should not primarily be around making money. The reason for this is that you are bound to make money (and lose it) whenever you buy, trade, and invest in stocks.

What your goal should be must revolve around longevity. You have to stay in the market for as long as possible to truly understand how it works. By understanding how things work in the market, you will have an easier time taking advantage of changes in it.

This is rather crucial especially in those conditions where losses are constant. Nearly every investor will have to deal with a losing streak for reasons that are outside or within their control. With a bit of self-discipline on your part, you can survive under these conditions with most of your capital intact and in a position to start profiting at the next upturn.

B. Tools and Assets

Now that the more personal stuff is out of the way, it is time to look into the things that you could personally arm yourself with to remain competitive in the market. The tools of a stock market investor can vary from person to person.

But, to keep things simple, here are some of the tools and assets that you should get acquainted with before you start investing.

1. Capital

It goes without saying but you should never venture into the stock market without a solid financial plan. The reason for this is that profiting in the market is not cut and dry. There is no assurance that you will be profiting here regularly but the chances of you losing money is always high. In short, you will not earn money in the stock market if you are not willing to spend the same or more in return.

It does not matter how much you have saved for stock investing, if we are to be honest about it. The point is that you should never become a stock investor on an empty wallet. But, just to be safe, save up to a $1,000.00 at the very least before you start investing.

2. A Trading Platform

A trading platform is simply the place where you do all your investment activities in. However, it is a rather crucial place to decide on before you step into the market. What you will have to consider here are the commissions offered or even the requirements necessary to access the platform.

There are brokers that use trading platforms that give high commissions for each trade but require a minimum account balance or a number of successful trades in the past in order to sign up in. In short, they may be good, but they are not ideal for absolute beginners like you.

Conversely, there are trading platforms out there that might work for your current setup. TD Ameritrade, for example, has no minimum account balance requirements although the commission you have to pay for your middlemen is quite high at $10.00 per trade. OptionHouse might be cheaper with a $5.00 trader's fee but more robust trading options and tools.

If you become more confident with your investing and trading skills, you can invest in more robust platforms like the Ameritrade one mentioned above or Interactive Brokers.

3. Mobile Apps

A serious investor and trader will have to take their work wherever they go. Fortunately, there are applications out that help you do all of your stock market activities in one handheld devices.

There are quite a lot of these apps out there which begs the question: What should you look for in them?

For starters, what you need is a diverse set of in-app tools and options. Choose an app that allows you to quickly search for and screen potential stock investments while also monitoring their performances in real time. If you want to be more advanced, choose an app that allows to you seamlessly move from your desktop computer to your handheld through a unified account system.

Lastly, choose an app with a reasonable subscription fee. Some mobile apps go for the $20.00 which might be pricey for some investors. If you do opt for an expensive app, make sure that you have access to a lot of features that will make your investment activities easier regardless of your location.

4. Stock Screening Tools

Looking for the stock that will fit your needs can be hard if you are a beginner. This is where a stock screener comes into play as it helps you look for stocks in the market based on a set of criteria that you yourself will determine.

For instance, you could be looking for stocks based on their market capitalization, the potential dividend yield, and the prices for each share being offered. Fortunately for you, most trading platforms and apps offer screeners as a basic feature.

However, there are dedicated screening apps out there like Finviz which offers more specific screening criteria. Of course, you will have to pay a subscription fee in order to get access for its advanced features but the basic services are free for all investors.

5. Charts, Charts, and More Charts

What you have to remember is that the stock market is not exactly the easiest thing to describe with mere words. The amount of number crunching and computations that happen here means that you are better off understanding the whole thing from a non-verbal viewpoint.

This is where charts come into play as it helps determine what actions to take by laying and connecting different points of data in a relatively easy to understand format. A simple look at a chart will tell you where a company is going performance wise, where the value of their stock prices are currently, what trend it is following, and what might happen in that sector within the next few hours or so.

Here's the caveat, though. It's a bit hard to understand these charts if you don't know what to look for and what each term means. Also, do keep in mind that these figures will change by the minute which means that stock charts have relatively short lifespans as far as relevance is concerned.

Fortunately, there are different services out there that will help you understand what the figures are saying in the simplest terms possible. It is up to you to get subscribed to them so you know how stocks are performing in real time.

6. Brokerages

Consider this one as the training wheels for every newbie stock investor. Since you are new to the market, there is always a chance that you might get confused and make mistakes in your activities. You can mitigate this by getting subscribed to a brokerage service who will assist you in getting a hand of the stocks that you want.

However, brokers require a fee which means a portion of your earnings will ultimately end up being used to pay other people. You can lessen your costs by looking for a discount brokerage which can offer all the basic amenities at a fraction of the price.

As of now, the best brokerages are Robinhood, TD Ameritrade, and Fidelity. E-Trade is also good if you are looking for a brokerage that can focus solely on buying and selling stocks. The point is that there are actually services out there that are inexpensive yet effective. The less money you will have to pay for good services, the more money you could use to go through the market.

7. Portfolio Analysis

Aside from the diversity of your investment portfolio, you also need to determine the risks and opportunities that are present with it. Portfolio analysis will help you go through all of your investments and understand which ones possess the best possible yields given the current market conditions.

However, the problem with a portfolio analysis is that they are rather expensive. That is if you don't know where to look for free services.

Portfolio Visualizer is a website that will offer a free analysis of your portfolio using data models that go several decades back. Their services will help you run simulations, find points of interest base on historical data, and test all current investments using a number of calculation tools.

The process might be intimidating to some but the results they produce are rather easy to understand. You can also use the data being given to you to further optimize your portfolio as a whole instead of looking at it by individual investments.

8. Financial Ratios

Stock market data are mostly numbers based. This is why the first order of the day for any investor is to make sense of every financial data being provided to them, A financial ratio will help you do just that while also locating and isolating those bits of information that you need the most. In essence, they help you understand the figures as a collective and as individual strands of data.

Financial ratios are quite diverse but they often fall under the same categories which are the following.

Price

As the name would imply, these ratios assess stocks according to their price. More often than not, you can use them to track the performance of a company since prices rise and fall according to how good a company is in that period.

As such, Price Ratios can use a number of models which include:

- Price to Earnings
- Price to Sales
- Price to Book
- Dividend Yield
- Dividend Payout

Profitability

Like the Price Ratio, Profitability Ratios track a company's performance. But, instead of the changes in their stock prices, this ratio determines performance by how a company earns comparative to the expenses they made. As such, profitability ratios use the following metrics:

- Profit Margin
- Return on Equity
- Return on Assets

Liquidity

This metric is used to determine how good a company is meeting short-term goals and obligations. You have to remember that companies tend to create debt just to function properly. Thus, what separates a good company from the rest is its ability to pay out such obligations as soon as possible.

A company that has low liquidity tends to create more debt or, worse, make decisions to raise money that does not bode well for the company in the long-term. In short, liquidity will tell you how well a company manages itself under tough financial conditions.

Under this ratio, the metrics below will be used:
- Current

- Quick

Debt

This ratio focuses more on how a company manages its obligations on a long-term basis. By looking at its starting capital and current financial structure, this ratio will help you understand the overall health of a company which indirectly tells you of their validity as an investment option.

With this ratio, the following metrics are to be used:

- Debt to Equity
- Interest Coverage

Efficiency

Under this ration, a company will be assessed on how it uses its capital and assets in order to function properly. It is mostly a management issue but this metric will help you determine just how good a company uses the investments it makes while also delivering on the promises it has made on investors. When using efficiency, the following will be looked into:

- Turnover of Assets
- Turnover of Inventory

Important Reminder: Do keep in mind that these ratios just tell you what MIGHT happen with a company based on currently available data, and know what will happen. As such, do not be dependent on them for information but do refer to them when making crucial investment decisions.

9. Budgeting and Portfolio Management

Although not exactly a tool for your investment activities, budgeting software will help you track how much you are spending on your activities and how much you have left on your current capital.

A budgeting software should help you manage your payments while checking on the prices of stocks.

As such, here are some of the budgeting apps that you should look into.

- **BlackGold -** This financing app will focus more on the prices of commodities like oil. It checks mostly for the prices of gasoline as well as the stocks of energy companies on a statewide and international basis.
- **PageOnce -**This app helps you keep track of all due bills **in** your investment and track their performance. It can send out regular

notifications to inform you of an upcoming payment so you wouldn't miss out.

- **Venmo -** This app helps you do all of your payments on one platform. It links to your existing investment accounts and bank numbers and sports an interface that is ideal for those new to investing. Also, it's free.
- **Wikinvest Portfolio -** A mobile portfolio analysis tool of sorts, this app helps you keep track of how your investments are faring in the market. It will import brokerage information and provide news on investors as they happen in real time.

10. A News Source

As was stated earlier, knowledge is crucial in order to survive as a stock investor. And any knowledge is not enough, however. It has to be up to date and based on the most accurate of figures.

Being subscribed to a news source is a must for any investor as this allows you to know what is happening in the market, which stocks are going up, and why. Of course, this is only effective if coupled with a habit of reading the news before you start the day,

Nevertheless, knowing what is new in your market is important as a stock investor. Fortunately, there are quite a lot of news sources out there that you could subscribe to and they tend to get updated on an hourly basis.

C. Technical Analysis Tools

Due to how robust their features are, it is best to separate these tools as their own category. The ability to accurately evaluate stock market data is crucial for any stock market investor. It removes a bit of the uncertainty that comes with investing while also preventing you from being too rash with your investment decisions.

Fortunately, technical analysis tools are readily available for all investors and traders right now. Yes, some might charge a free for premium features but most do not require you to pay up just to enjoy the bare essentials.

Brokers

A lot of brokerage firms right now provide technical analysis tools to ease in newcomers in the field. They mostly draw their data from Recognia, a Canadian Third Party company that provides stock market data for a lot of trading platforms and brokers.

By analyzing changes in the price of stocks, Recognia will give investors and traders the insight needed to see if certain stock options are worth the while to invest in or not. Recognia itself is not available for those who are not operating brokerages. However, you can be certain that most of these brokerages who offer technical analysis will have Recognia incorporated into their services.

- **Charles Schwab**

This broker operates a trading platform named StreetSmart Edge. This platform, in turn, analyzes data being streamed in real time which allows users to go through stocks and ETFs with the already existing Screener Plus feature. The platform also provides a number of charts which track the progress of the stocks you were looking for in real time. You can customize what each chart would present based on several parameters.

- **E-Trade**

E-Trade uses a system called the Live Action Scanner. As the name would imply, it scans the market in real-time for stock prices as well as analyze technical information that would affect any changes to such. It is also a rather robust screening feature as it uses at least 100 pre-defined screening options that investors can mix and match.

Also, the scanner can do a portfolio analysis for you by tracking which of the investments you have made were overbought, underbought, dropping, or rising in prices. And if one of your stocks meets criteria you yourself have set in the scanner, the program will alert you. On paper, this should help you adjust your strategies in response to those changes.

- **Fidelity Investments**

This broker uses the Active Trader Pro system which can track stocks in real time and alert you of any changes in the stocks that you have invested in or are planning to. For instance, if a stock in a company is open for trading, the system will alert you if you have tagged that company previously.

There is also an advanced charting option that lets you peer way back several decades of a company's stock history. If you want something more recent, the system can also track changes that have occurred in the past month or, better yet, in the past 60 minutes.

And if that is not enough, Fidelity Ivnestments does offer several online courses through the system that help traders get a handle of their technical analysis tools as well as improve on their stock strategies.

- **Interactive Brokers**

What Interactive Brokers have that others have yet to offer is a more extensive charting option. Using the data that they got with Recognia and pairing that up with hundreds of performance indicators, what IB gives to investors is the chance to really see how stocks have performed or are performing based on a number of criteria that they prefer.

Also, you can use your IB account and attach it to a third=party analytics tool. In theory, this should allow you to chart stocks in a manner that truly fits your overall investment strategy.

- **Lightspeed**

Catering to day traders, Lightspeed uses a scanner called LightScan to search and filter through hundreds of trading options. How it works is that goes through multiple markets looking for the stocks that will meet the criteria you have set in the program.

The program can also chart up to 20 years of historical stock data to give you an idea as to how certain stocks have been performing in multiple market conditions. The entire program is still in beta as of now but you can download the demo if you want to try things out for yourself.

- **Thinkorswim**

The trading platform of TD Ameritrade,
Thinkorswim is primarily catered for options
trading but it has some features that do make
things easier for equity traders as well. In here,
you will find several drawing tools, data
visualization tools, and hundreds of technical
indicators.

What Thinkorswim does is it allows traders to
create their own analysis scheme in order to
analyze stocks based on criteria that they think
works for them best. Thinkorswim is best used
on the desktop as the mobile version has some
optimization issues.

- **TradeStation**

Out of all the broker-based technical analysis
tools out there, TradeStation is perhaps the one
that was designed for technical analysis from the
ground up. It traces its origins from the software
made by the Omega Research firm which should
tell you that this was designed specifically to
analyze stock options.

TradeStation offers an automated analysis
feature that monitors trade stocks in real time. It
also sports an AI which seemingly adjusts its
monitoring in response to the criteria you often
use in previous activities. It's charting feature
can also draw from several decades of historical

data while also simulating future stock performances.

Standalone Programs and Websites

- **ESignal**

.The most current iteration, ESignal 12, is a downloadable program that comes with a number of technical analysis and consultation packages. It is also compatible with the services offered by Tradier and Interactive Brokers which makes this a handy inclusion if you already use those services already.

The downside? ESignal is rather expensive. The basic version is $54.00 per month and comes with a paltry 25 technical analysis features and a 15-minute delay in data streaming. If you want a more real-time streaming service and several hundreds of data analysis services, you must pay for the Signature version which comes at a whopping $176.00 per month.

- **iVest MarketGear**

This program sports charting features that allow you to track stocks using customizable performance indicators. Aside from that, you can use drawing tools to determine market trends, look back on all the past trades you have made, and schedule when and how you are going to start trading certain stocks.

The basic version offers 100 technical indicators that should help you find the stocks that meet your preferences. Also, MarketGear sports compatibility with TD Ameritrade, and E-Trade. As for subscription fees, you only have to deal with a $38.00 per month price tag.

- **Meta Stock**

Having been in the market since the 1980s, Meta Stock is one of the oldest technical analysis tools for traders and investors out there. There are a number of versions of the tool available in the market right now but the best one happens to be Meta Stock R/T which features real-time analysis and tracking.

The basic version comes with 150 performance indicators plus a number of interpretations to help you understand what each indicator is telling you. If you opt for the advanced version, Meta Stock comes with an Indicator Builder feature that lets you create your own indicators. In theory, this means that you should be able to come up with analysis based on strategies of your own making or for those that the tools were primarily designed for.

Subscription comes at $100.00 per month and data live feeds are purely optional. Also, Meta

Stock is quite compatible with Interactive Brokers.

- **TC2000**

Known formerly as Worden's TC2000, this program is compatible with a number of operating systems and can be linked to the Interactive Brokers system. It's the most basic package, the practice version, which allows for charting, screening, and trade monitoring. It is also free to download.

However, if you want to have access to more scanning options and performance indicators, you will have to get the gold and platinum versions which are priced at $30.00 and $80.00 per month respectively. Data feeds have also be paid separately. Regardless of this steep asking price, the TC2000 system has been known to be rather dependable for investors looking at stock performance under specific market conditions.

The Habits of Highly Successful Investors

Having the right tools and qualities will be enough in order to succeed, right? Not quite. You see, these assets, tools, and personal qualities are good but only if they manifest into something actionable. And the manifestation should not be a one-time thing but must be executed on a daily basis.

In other words, arming yourself with the right skills and tools is not enough if you don't actually use them on a constant basis. Sustaining this effort is thus the key to becoming successful as an investor.

As such, you need to develop habits that increase your chances of success as an investor. These habits include:

1. **Saving Money**

Regardless of your intended strategy as an investor and then as a trader, you should never come to the market with less than the ideal amount you have set up for your investing activities. Remember that you are going to spend here in order to earn more which is why you need a sizeable capital to sustain your efforts.

So what's the ideal amount that you should have saved before becoming a stock market investor? There is no exact figure but the generally accepted figure would be 15% of your yearly income. Of course, that is the baseline as some people would actually put off more than 20% before starting on their careers as investors.

Whatever the case, it is important that you must have more than a few hundred dollars saved up for investments if you want to be in the market for as long as possible.

2. Diversify

Risk is something that you will have to deal with regularly as an investor. It may be something light as sudden but minor changes in company performances to drastic ones like massive economic downturns.

There is no escaping risk in stock investing but you can soften its blow by spreading your activities in different sectors and stock types. Diversification works by adding new stock types from different fields to your investment portfolio.

The goal here is to create a safety net that will prevent your entire portfolio from losing value in case one industry falls. For example, let say that there are two investors, A and B. Both of them have invested $1,000.00 in stocks. A invested all of it in crude oil and metal. B, on the other hand, invested in energy, electronics, finance, real estate, and retail.

Now, if stock prices were to drop in the oil and metals scene, A has a greater risk of losing all of his $1,000.00. B, on the other hand, might lose some of his money if the sectors he invested in took a turn for the worse but not all of his money will go to waste if the other sectors continue performing well.

Of course, diversification does not guarantee profit nor does it ensure that you will not suffer a loss. At the very least, it lessens the blow if things get worst The best part is that diversification does not work on a per-stock-class basis. You can further diversify stocks in their own categories. Some smart investors do diversify according to investment types, geographic location, size, and stock exposure.

3. Sticking to a Plan (Despite Market Volatility)

When the value of an investment falls, it is natural to entertain thoughts of bailing out. A good investor, on the other hand, resists such an urge.

Instead of taking their money and running with it, an investor will maintain a sizeable allocation of stocks that can help them live regardless of the market condition. When the financial crisis of 2008 happened, a lot of investors scrambled to get the most of their money before things eventually went south.

Although they might have recovered a portion of what they invested, they had a harder time starting from scratch when things picked up again in the early 2010s. In fact, those that did not panic in '08 were able to maintain a presence in the market even as things got worse until 2010. But when things got better, they were the first to open themselves to better trading and investment options.

This habit tends to go along with a diversified investment portfolio. The point is that you do not bail out when things get worse. Instead, you adjust your strategies so that you can still meet your goals even when the market is in a downturn phase.

4. Focusing on After-Tax Returns

The taxes you have to pay often affect how much you can earn from your investments, depending on the situation. As such, you should consider adding in options that yield higher after-tax returns to get the most out of your investment. For example, a 401K, an IRA, and other annuities can generate higher after-tax returns due to their nature.

You should also learn how to perform asset location and account location. The former is the practice of putting in your investments on different accounts based on their tax treatment and efficiency. The latter, on the other hand, focuses more on putting your investment on accounts depending on how taxes are treated in them.

In practice, this means putting in your investments with the least amount of tax efficiencies like bonds in accounts that are tax-deferred by nature such as an IRA or a 401K. On the other hand, if the investment is more tax-efficient, you must place them in a taxable account.

Taxes should not be the sole focus of your investment decisions, mind you. This is habit is purely effective in making sure that you get the most of your investments while still complying with tax laws. And we know how much Internal Revenue can be ruthless when it comes to getting the government's share in personal profit.

To Conclude

Now, does having the right skills, mindset, assets, tools, and strategies lead to a successful investor? Not exactly. Remember that there is no assurance of success in the stock market. Everyone gets the same opportunities and deal with the same threats. It is up to the individual stock investor to play to their strengths and take advantage of changes in a situation.

That being said, it does not hurt to arm yourself with the best possible tools in the industry to increase your chances of succeeding. You may not even use all the tools mentioned here or even use strategies outside of this book. The point is that your creativity and persistence will play a huge role in becoming successful as an investor.

With all of those out the way, let us begin preparing you for making your first steps into the market.

Chapter V: Buying Your First Stock

As of this point, we have only talked about what you must be and what you must have in order to succeed as an investor. But there is still one question that remains to be answered:

What should you DO in order to succeed in the stock market?

Do not get the idea that this is a rather easy question to answer. In fact, it's a rather loaded one, and how you answer it depends greatly on how well you applied all that you have learned so far. As such, from this point on, we are going to talk about how you could make the best of your time whenever you are in the stock market.

To start things off, let's focus on actually acquiring stocks and other investment options. Here's how.

1. Finding a Broker

Now, we've talked exhaustively about the different brokers that you can subscribe to as an investor. However, that still does not answer the question as to which brokerage firm will be best for you. Keep in mind that the best ones cater to different styles and needs.

Also, do remember that commission is no longer a problem when it comes to some brokerage firms like Charles Schwab and TD Ameritrade since they have already removed that. In other words, the cost is not exactly going to be your biggest concern for and the rest of the foreseeable future.

As such, you ought to ask yourself a few questions when you pick a broker.

A. **Do They Have All that You Need?**

When you ask this question, you should look be focusing on the services that they offer. For example, a broker might be content in providing you with more investment options which is why they might offer trading options in foreign stock markets or the option to buy fractional shares in a company.

Other companies might want to invest in your development which is why they also want to make you a better trader/investor. Some brokers offer educational programs, sources, weekly newsletters, and other information sources that you can draw a lot of knowledge from.

Each broker has its own set of features and advantages on offer. As a rule of thumb, you must pick the one who's promised amenities are worth the subscription fee that you will eventually pay for.

B. Are They Easy to Deal With?

Assuming that you are going to be tech-savvy and do all of your investing and trading in multiple devices, you need a broker whose platform is optimized for handheld devices. It's a common feature nowadays for brokers to allow investors and traders to do on-button transactions which should speed up the process without sacrificing comfort and safety.

One other aspect you could look into here is navigation. A good brokerage platform should allow for seamless transitions between pages and processes so that you don't have to go back frequently just to make sure that your information is correct.

Also, check if that brokerage firm allows for "trial phases" for their programs. This is not a chance for you to test the quality of the broker for free but to also get comfortable with how things are done in the platform.

But if you are a stock investor/trader that is not comfortable with doing all your activities online, then find a broker with a physical branch near where you live. This should reduce a lot of time fumbling through pages and charts while also getting direct, uninterrupted consultation with a broker.

C. Narrowing the Field

Now that you know what you need and intend to do with the help of a broker, the next thing to do is to limit your choices down to a handful. Every broker has its own features, advantages, and disadvantages but a good one tends to check certain boxes which include:

- Membership at a Stock Broker Regulation and Trust firm like the Securities Investor Protection Corporation.
- Membership at the Financial Industry Regulation Authority.
- Coverage from the Federal Insurance Corporation especially if they offer Cash Deposit, Money Market Deposit Accounts, and other similar accounts.
- Insurance amounting to $250,000.00 at the very least in case of problems.
- Fraud Protection guarantees
- Account protection protocols to prevent online attacks.
- A consistent customer review score ranging from good to above average

What all of these qualities imply is that the firm knows how to facilitate your online activities for you without leaving you unnecessarily exposed to threats coming from outdoor threats and even in-door system deficiencies. After all, you are dealing with huge amounts of money here which is why you'd rather do it on a secure platform.

2. Opening an Account

Once you have found the brokerage that fits your style and needs the most, the next step is to actually open up an account in their firm. It is a fairly straightforward process and will involve you disclosing certain basic yet vital information about yourself.
What that in mind, it is still best that you take into consideration a few points.

A. How Are You Going to Be Funded/Paid?

As of now, there are multiple ways to funnel money in and out of your brokerage account. When opening an account, do consider the following options:

- **Electronic Funds Transfer -** This is one of the more convenient options as it connects your account to an already existing checking or saving account that you already have. At best, the funds that you have wired will show up at the account on the next business day.
- **Wire Transfer -** This is a direct bank to bank transaction which would mean it takes minutes for a single transaction to be

completed. If you are looking for a fast transaction, this option is the best for you.

- **Checks -** One of the more variable funding options, checks do not allow for instant transmission of money but trades it for a more secure transaction. Of course, the availability of funds in an account is never assured but, at the very least, you can demand payment if that check does bounce.
- **Assets Transfer -** This option is ideal if you have more than 401K in your account or intend to transfer investments that you already have to another broker.
- **Stock Certificates -** You are not exactly transferring money here but direct ownership of the stock. If you have a paper certificate and want to trade that stock to another, you can have the certificate mailed into an online account. It's not the most efficient funding option but it does work.

B. What Privileges are Being Offered?

Privileges are simply the incentives that you are bound to enjoy in consideration of opening up an account with that firm. These benefits are divided into two groups which are:

- **Margin Privileges**

These benefits provide the ability for an account holder to borrow money from the firm in order to buy stocks. Investing on a margin is not always a good path to take but having margin privileges can help you get out of a bind.

For example, there are some instances where you cannot use the funds you deposited unless you opened a margin account. If this requirement is present in your account, then have a margin account opened but make sure that whatever amount you borrowed will be paid in time.

- **Options Trading Privileges**

Stock options are generally best avoided if you are a new trader but it would be best to know if you have options trading privileges being offered by the firm. Do not worry as there are several levels of options trading privileges that you can choose from. You can even change such privileges once you get used to being an investor/trader.

3. Research

This is where the bulk of your time buying your first stock should be focused. In no circumstance should you go in on an investment blind. Instead, you should know everything that is to possibly know about that stock before you purchase them.

And that does give rise to the question: What should you look for when going through investment options. Here are some factors to consider.

A. Earnings Growth

First things first, you have to determine how well the value of those stocks has increased over the years. What you should be looking for here is not one-time, massive changes but a gradual improvement of value over time. A "trend", if you will.

Use your broker platforms and see if they can plot a chart on the price of that stock for years. What you should be looking for is an upwards trend. There might be drops occurring through the years but it should generally follow a path where the value now is quite better than what that company had at the start.

Once you know that that stock follows an upwards trend, the next thing to find out is why. As a rule, always pick company whose stocks enjoyed upwards value trend is sparked by changes in the quality of their products and/.or services. This is an indicator of strong performance and viability.

B. Relative Company Strength

When looking for a company to purchase stocks at, you have to first look at the industry it operates in. Normally, a strong industry performance will tell you that a company will thrive there.

But, of course, you have to know how that company is performing relative to its competitors. What advantages does it have? Has it used those advantages or played to its strengths? Is there a potential threat to its viability to you as an investment? These are crucial questions that you need to be asking as you'd rather invest in a competitive company than a failing one (unless that's your strategy, of course).

To evaluate a company's relative strength, you have to look at its sales figures as well as its cash flows and income statement. You can make this easier for yourself by lining up that company with its competitors and gauging how it is performing compared to the rest for a certain time period. There are broker apps out that there that can help you draw this performance up quickly.

C. Debt to Equity Ratio
Out of all the financial ratios that you can use, this is perhaps the most crucial when looking for stocks to buy. To use this, you have to get a hold of the company's income statement. If you have the figures, you have to divide the total liabilities

that a company has in its sheet by the total number of shareholders.

If you are looking for a company with a low risk tolerance, the figure that you should come up with should be no more than 0.3, Of course, this debt to equity ratio works for most companies not all. Construction firms, for instance, have higher debt to equity ratios due to their reliance on funding incurred by debts.

Whatever the case, just make sure that that company's debt to equity ratio falls within the norms of the industry that they are part in. At the very least, a good debt to equity ratio tells you that the company, if things get worst, will have more shareholders to pay than creditors.

D. Price to Earnings Ratio

As the name would imply, this ratio determines how much a company's price in its stocks is doing compared to how much it has been earning. As a matter of fact, this ratio will tell you if a company is either overvalued or undervalued.

To find this ratio, what you will have to do is to divide the company's current share price by the price of its earnings per share. For example, if a company is trading it's stocks for $30.00 per share and it's   earnings per share is at $1.875, then the price to earnings ratio is at 16 which is a rather strong figure.

You can even use this ratio to compare stock prices between competing companies I the same sector.

E. Dividends Management

To be straight to the point, a company should be paying its dividends in order to be seen as a stable company to invest in. This is quite important if that company has shown an increase in payout over several years. In other words, it is earning more than enough to pay itself, its staff, and then all those shareholders who invested in it.

Here's a caveat, though: that an increase in dividend yield should not be sudden so as to form a spike in the chart. That is a rather telltale sign that the company is not investing in itself much or is getting desperate in reeling in new investors.

Also, the dividend yield is not always necessary to determine how good a company is performing. When the economic times get hard, it is common for companies to cut on their dividends in order to stay afloat. It's not a sign that the company is about to go under but, rather, it is shifting its goals so that creditors are paid first and its employees are taken care of.

But, if the conditions are good in the economy, then look for a strong dividend payout when investing.

F. The Leadership

You have to know exactly WHO runs the company. Effective leadership means that that company can last long in different economic conditions while managing a stable flow of income.

Aside from having a strong baseline performance in leadership, the executives must also show signs of innovation as well as flexibility in the markets that they choose to operate in. Under the best conditions, this means that the company's stocks are not only following an upwards trend in price but that the trend itself is being charted on a higher point than most of its competitors.

G. Long-Term Stability

If there is one term that you need to really understand when it comes to the stock market, it would be volatility. Nothing is ever certain here and what performs well today will be losing hundreds or thousands of dollars a few hours later. That's the rather peculiar dynamic in the market that everyone else has to keep up with.

As such, do not make profit as your sole factor in determining a company's strength. Eventually, every company is going to lose value in the stock market for reasons within and outside of its control. What you should be looking for, on the other hand, is a company's stability in the market over a long-term basis.

This should be reflected in your chart as a smooth yet upwards trend. It may hit a few downturns here and there but the company should be able to pull itself back together and come back stronger than ever.

This should also be reflected in a number of factors we have already discussed in this section. A stable company has strong revenues, low debt levels, a strong competitive advantage, and is ran by people who exactly know what they are doing.

4. Deciding on Share Quantity

Now that you know what company to invest in, the next part would be determining how many shares you'd want to purchase. Compared to the previous step, this should be a rather straightforward process so there should be no pressure on your part on how many stocks you'd want to buy.

But what is a good range for newbie investors like you? Just to be safe, start with the smallest quantifiable number out there: 1.

Starting with just one share does have its benefits. For starters, it helps you get the feel of that company without overly exposing yourself to risk if you happen to buy at an inopportune time. Once you feel confident with that company, you can add in more stocks,

You may also want to consider what are called as "Fractional Shares". This is something new in companies where you get to buy a portion of a share, not the full thing. The advantage they have to offer is they allow investors to get a hold of more expensive stocks without having to go over their budget,

However, not all brokers offer this option. Only a few brokers like Charles Schwab, SoFi Active Investing, and Robinhood offer these fractional shares, Either way, it is recommended that you ask if such an option is offered by your broker. On paper, they would allow you to earn more stocks, pay for the entire stock gradually, and diversify your portfolio in an instant.

5. Choosing Your Stock Order Type

This is one of the more deceptive parts of the buying process not because it is actually easy. Instead, the opposite applies as choosing the right stock order type for you looks complicated but, in application, is one of the easiest parts of the process.

How so? For starters, you are going to be encountering a lot of fancy words and terms that companies call their stock orders with. You might start thinking that you are now going to deal with a lot of complicated trading jargon just to get survive in this field.

The truth? You don't need to learn a lot of complicated order types and terms just to successfully buy stock. In fact, a lot of successful investors made careers for themselves buying two order types only. They are as follows.

A. **Market Order**

A market order is simply the type where you buy the stock at its best and current available price in the market. One notable advantage that this stock order type has is that it allows for immediate execution and fulfillment of your order. The reason for this is that there is no price parameters set for the purchase. Of course, the order is immediately executed if you are not buying shares worth over millions or are taking part in a shift of majority votes in a company.

However, since there are no price parameters, do expect that the price that you are given will not be the same price quoted to you when you were contemplating buying that stock a few moments ago. Bidding and selling prices would actually fluctuate by the hour. As such, a market order is great if you are ordering stocks with more stable price swings.

In other words, this order type is great if you are buying stock from a larger, reputable, and stable company.

Protip: Timing is the key to making the most of a market order since prices fluctuate by the hour. As such, do your market order "after hours". this means that you must purchase the stock when the stock market has closed for the day.

Why? This will cause your order's price to be placed at the most prevailing price of that stock for the day when the stock exchange opens for the next day. So as long as the prevailing price was good on that day, you can be sure of a rather good purchase price for your stocks.

Also, do check the terms of execution by the trader of your choice in this order type. Some brokers that offer their stocks cheap will often bundle all the orders of their customers and execute them all at once under that stock's prevailing price for the day. At least, you'd know why your stock orders are taking so long to be executed if ever that happens.

B. Limit Order

Unlike the market order, limit orders give investors and traders better control over the price range of stock. How it works is quite simple.

Let us say, for example, that company DEF is trading their stocks at $200.00 per share. However, you think that the stocks should be priced at $180.00 given the performance of the company currently. Add to that, there is a chance that the price would drop at $180.00 or below within the next few hours or days.

As such, a limit order works by telling the trader to hold off on executing the trade with you until the price drops to $180.00. Think of it like going to the department store and telling the cashier to place all your orders in a secret compartment so you could pay for them once the shop has a sale.

This type of order is quite favorable for investors that want to invest in smaller and more volatile companies or when the market is experiencing some short-term volatility period.

Also, you can even further customize your limit order by adding certain conditions. You can go for an All or None Order where your order will be executed only when all the shares that you wish to buy have reached a certain price point.

Alternatively, you could for the Good for the Day type where your order will either be executed or expire at the end of the day even if not all conditions are met. Lastly, you can go for the Good Til Canceled type where your order will never expire until you say so or 2 to 4 months have passed and the stocks have not met your conditions.

Other Points to Consider

Keep in mind that a limit order does not exactly guarantee the fulfillment of your order. The order type actually operates on a first-come-first-served basis. The orders that have parameters that are easier to complete will be fulfilled first and will only happen if the trade actually benefits the trader as well.

Also, a limit order can be more costly to an investor in the long run. Limit orders that were not completed or fulfilled for a day may continue on being fulfilled in the next few days which can increase costs on your part. As such, temper your conditions with the actual figures in the market. The more feasible your conditions are, the quicker it is for your limit order to be fulfilled.

If all goes well and you follow all of the steps above, then Congratulations! You have finally purchased your first stock. Now, the question is what will you do with it?

An investor has several options on what they could do with their stocks in the foreseeable future. We will discuss them intently in the chapters to follow.

Chapter VI: The Basics of Trading

As was previously stated, trading is perhaps one of the quicker methods to earn from your stay in the stock market. But just because you own stocks does not mean that you have what it takes to be a successful trader.

There is an art as well as a science to trading your stocks. Depending on your chosen strategy, the entire process could be a breeze or a total hectic nightmare on your part.

But since it is an integral part of the stock market, it pays to know just what it takes to succeed in the field of trading stocks. Aside from that, you should know how to manage some of the more inherent risks and opportunities within this sub-field of the market. Here's how.

The Basics

Since this will be your inaugural attempt at trading, it is best to keep things nice and simple. That being said, the entire process of trading stocks can be broken down into a handful of steps.

1. Owning a Brokerage Account

It goes without saying that you can't trade if you are not affiliated with a brokerage firm. The previous chapter has gone into considerable detail on the intricacies of opening one up so you should know how to do one for yourself now.

That being said, this is the easy part as you are merely setting up the platform where you are going to do all of your trading-related activities.

2. Understanding Market and Limit Orders from a Trader's Perspective

"Haven't we discussed this already? You may ask and, yes, that is true,

But what you have understood so far as market and limit orders are concerned is how they work from a buyer's point of view. What about the trader, then?

As with a buyer, a trader can choose to use limit or market orders depending on what they want. However, there are some key advantages that a trader can get from these order types which are as follows.

A. **Market Orders -** Since these order types require that an order be executed ASAP, you can actually determine when that day will that order be executed. This works in two ways. First, it helps you take advantage of the prevailing price of that stock so you also get to profit considerably from the trade. That is, of course, if the order was done before the exchange closes for that day.

As a matter of fact, you can have all orders executed at any time of the day that you want so that you don't spend all day doing repeated order fulfillment processes. At the very least, this is a more convenient order type for you.

But what about "after hours" trades? Well, the prices of those stocks will be fixed at the prevailing price for that day which will be used as a baseline for the next day when the exchange opens.

Also, the price that the stock will be bought for may not exactly be the same as the price that you quoted to the buyer. Depending on the time when the trade was done, this might work to your advantage.

B. **Limit Orders -** Due to the placing of parameters for the execution of stock, you might think that this order type would not e beneficial to you. However, this also means that you have more control over how the order is going to be fulfilled.

If the buyer, for example, places a condition that the order will be fulfilled if 20% of stock prices drop before a certain period but another buyer will purchase the same stocks ASAP, you can at least put more preference in the latter instead of the former.

In essence, you get to dictate who can purchase your stocks and in what period depending on which buyers have the least amount of "demands" before they start paying up for certain stocks.

3. Practice

Arguably, there is a certain level of intimidation when it comes to trading. You can soften your entry into the process by going for some low-pressure practice rounds with the brokerage firm of your choice. Some firms like TD Ameritrade and Interactive Brokers allow for first-time traders to do some "paper trading" transactions where you trade actual yet low-priced stocks for a small amount of money or none at all.

The goal in these practice trades is to let you hone your skills in trading without putting a serious dent in your budget. Also, it helps you build your record as a trader so that other buyers will have more confidence in doing business with you.

Just to be safe, ask for this option from the brokerage of your choice. Some do not offer practice trading opportunities but offer alternatives like training courses and consultation.

4. Benchmarking

The goal for trading stocks is to always be a few steps ahead of a certain performance index. So what exactly is a "Performance Index"? It could simply be the index used by Standard & Poor known as the 500 Index. It could also be the composite index used by NASDAQ. It could be any of those smaller performance indexes used by agencies and focusing on certain factors like geographical location, size, and industry type.

Whatever the case, you should have a good idea of how the market is faring as of this minute. If an investor you are dealing with is not able to keep up with that performance benchmark, then you should aim for low-cost investment options like mutual funds or ETFs. The point is that the stocks that you have to offer for that day must align with what the benchmark index is telling you will be profitable for that day.

5. Trade!

If you are ready to place in your first trade,all you will have to do is fund your brokerage account through the funding system you have placed for it. If the funds are already processed and ready for use, you will then have to select the stock that you want to trade, pick the type of order you want to use, and then place your order.

What is important here is that you make sure that the order actually executes. A market order will be processed immediately while a limit order takes a good bit of time to get processed. As such, try to make your parameters a bit more reasonable and achievable so that your limit order will be processed quicker.

Survival Tips for Beginners

Your ability to go through the trading process safely is a hallmark of a good trader. Things can get rather "intense" when trading. In fact, it is at trading where that misconception of the stock market being ruthless could be traced from.

However, that does not mean that absolute rookies like you can't survive their first stint at the trading process. Here's how:

1. Build Your Base Slowly and Gradually

Look, you must never come to the trading process with guns blazing. That's a surefire way of getting yourself into a position where you are going to lose a lot of money from more experienced traders and buyers. Get the feel of the process first by doing some low-cost activities like:

- **Dollar-Cost Averaging:**

Here, you are only controlling yourself on how much you will trade and when you will trade. The set amount will be what you will use to buy shares when stock prices are low and fewer when prices rise. The point is that your costs will even out after a period of time has elapsed.

Here's an example to make things easier to understand. Let us say that you have a budget of $1,000.00 per month for investing. When you apply dollar-cost averaging, here's what your budget will look like:

- Month 1: $30.00. Hence, $1,000 divided by $30.00 will be 33 shares.
- Month 2: $25.00. Hence, $1,000 divided by $25.00 will be 40 shares
- Month 3: $20.00. Hence, $1,000 divided by $20.00 will be 50 shares
- Month 4: $50.00. Hence, $1,000 divided by $50.00 will be 20 shares
- Month 5: $40.00. Hence, $1,000 divided by $40.00 will be 25 shares

Within 5 months of using the system, you would have acquired 168 unique shares without overspending. You can do this by setting up a schedule for yourself but there are brokers out

there that can automate the scheduling process
for you.

- **Buying in Thirds**

Here, you will divide the amount you have set up
for trading by three and pick which of the three
areas you want to focus the most. You can either
choose for regular intervals like months or
quarters or on specific events like company
anniversaries or improvements in their
performance.

- **Basket Buying**

Now, what if you cannot decide which of the
several companies you have picked has the best
chances of success since both are equally viable?
The next best option is to buy or trade stocks
from both. This immediately takes the stress of
having to pick the best company to invest in
while also taking advantage of any sudden
changes in either company's performance.

This strategy is also great for determining which
of the two companies will eventually be the
better option so you could invest more in them.

2. Never, Ever Fall for a "Hot Tip"

There are a lot of pump and dump schemes out
there looking for suckers who would invest in
cheap stocks. They usually drum up hype in the

market (usually on the Internet) and even pay seemingly trustworthy Wall Street gurus to ensure that everything is okay.

Once they have enough investors, they would then drive prices up to attract more investors. If enough money has been generated, these people would then bail out of the market, sending all the prices of their stock crashing.

The point here is to never fall for any stock trading tip that assures you massive profit yields at a short amount of time and companies being backed by people you can't seemingly find notable credentials off in the Internet. A little bit of care and common sense will help in preventing you from becoming the next target of a stock market money trap.

3. Make Friends with the Tax Man

If you are trader that is not using a 401K or IRA account, then you are not enjoying a tax-favored status. This means that you are going to be taxed on your capital gains considerably which can complicate things.

However, the IRS does have different rules and tax rates depending on your income as well as well as the type of trading that you do. And if discrepancies do arise from the computation of your taxes, you can dispute such and present proof that you have only earned this much for that period. The excess that you have paid will then be off-set in the next tax period (refunds are not possible with the IRS, sadly).

4. **Don't Anticipate**

If you have made the decision to buy or trade stocks, you might feel the urge to get the orders done PRONTO. As such, you start watching the charts and wait for the right moment to pounce and purchase/trade those stocks.

This is where a lot of frustration as the charts might get close to your desired price but then drop down again. What you should be doing instead is find the "sweet spot" where the price is good enough for you and the buyer. It might not be close to what you want but, at least, you have a nice point of entry where you can start negotiations for the price of your stocks. If you wait too long to start trading, you might come to a point where the trend starts taking a downwards turn.

5. **Time it Right**

If the goal of the investor is to buy cheap, then a trader's goal is to buy and trade at the right time. So what is the "right time", exactly?

When you see that the stock is getting strong I.e. heading towards an upwards trend, then it is time to start buying. And if the stocks are showing signs of following a downwards trend, then it is time to sell.

The key emphasis here is that the stocks "show" either strength or weakness, not when they are actually strong and weak. if that happens, then the price is too costly for you or too low for you to make a profit when you want to start trading.

Here's an example. Suppose that the stocks of the company are at $10.00 per share but are going to $25.00 in the next few days due to strong performance. Don't wait for the stocks to actually reach $25.00 per share before you start buying. And if the reverse were to happen, don't wait for stock prices to go to the $10.00 mark before you start trading. At least, you won't put yourself at a disadvantage by timing your activities right.

Alternative Trading Strategies

If you have mastered the more basic concepts of trading, you might want to try out the other tactics that experienced traders have been using.

Everybody has their own way of going about trading stocks but which of these strategies have proven to work? Their effectiveness will vary depending on the situation but here are some of the tactics that experienced (and successful) traders have used in the past.

1. IPO

Known formally as Initial Public Offerings, IPOs are a direct consequence of a company shifting from a private firm to a publicly traded one. In most cases, the IPOs of a company is the first stocks that it offered to its first stockholders and can be traded publicly once the company enters the stock market.

Profiting from an IPO can be done in two ways. The first option is to watch and wait for how the value of these stocks changes as time goes by. If the price is fair given the circumstances, then buy it then wait for prices to go up to trade them again.

The second option is to buy the IPOs as soon as the company gets publicly traded. However, there is no assurance that the value of that stock will rise as it is dependent on the company's long-term and short-term performance rate. But, if the company does grow in the market, you can then sell the stocks at a higher price.

2. **The Short Sell**

This strategy is great for traders who are a bit adventurous with their activities. The entire premise of short selling is that you sell stocks (not owned by you) in the belief that their value will rapidly decline in a few weeks or days. And when that price drops massively, you can purchase them again at the new low price and return the stocks to their owners.

However, this trick only works if the stock in question actually drops. If the stock is poised for a drop but, instead, soars in price, you'd end up losing money. As such, the potential losses you can get from a short sell is greater than the potential gains you might generate. A bit of meticulous speculating will be necessary in order to make this strategy work.

3. **Trading by Margins**

If you have a margins account, you are given the option to borrow money so you could trade stocks. With the money you borrowed, you can increase the number of stocks that you can purchase without having to wait for additional funds to get wired into your account.

Here's an example. Let us say that the entire price for the 10 stocks you purchased is at $200.00. If you do not have a margins account, you are going to pay the total sum of money directly from the available amount in your account. But with the margins option, the stockbroker might lend you half or $100.00 while you supply the rest.

If your stocks yield a profit of $20.00 per stock which gives you a profit of $400.00. You return the $100.00 you owe to the stockbroker while you keep the rest of the money.

Here's a caveat, however. Do use the Margins Option only when you are in a pinch. It's easy to get reckless and abuse the option. What happens if stock prices drop and you actually generated losses? You are still obligated to pay the amount you owe to the broker.

Even More Advanced Strategies for Day Traders

Day trading is where things can get exciting. If you want to try your hand it is, you must understand that the overall goal for survival here is to find the best trend for the day and exit at the right moment.

So what makes for a good day trading tactic? It must follow certain elements like:

- **Trading Signals -** The strategy should clearly lay out how it is going to open and close trades. The clearer the technical rules will be, the easier it will be for you to implement them. And the more logical they are, the less room for interpretation and impulsiveness there will be on your part if you start trading.

- **Rules for Stop-Loss -** Risk is a definite factor in day trading and your goal is to mitigate much of it to the best of your ability. This is where a stop-loss rule comes in as a good one can limit the risk exposure of your investments to 1-2%. Any trader will have to do 50 to 100 losing trades in order to lose all of their funds in an account. How good would it be if those 50-100 bad trades were actually good ones? This only happens if you have a clear stop-loss rule and can follow it easily.

- **Moderate to High Success Rate -** The strategy you will use must have a success rate that is relatively high compared to the risk that you are going to expose yourself to it. In other words, the rewards that you are going to potentially get from it should be worth the risk that you will eventually suffer if things get out of hand.

For example, if you have a strategy with a success rate of 50%, then that means 5 out of 10 trades will be successful. Now, combine this with a risk to return ratio of 1 to 10 where there is 1 risky trade for every 9 moderately risky trades. That means that in 50% of all trades, you will guess correctly.

Just keep in mind that you are still crunching numbers as of this part.   There is no telling how every trade will happen. Whatever the case, your discipline as a trader, and your ability to exit before losses start piling up will be crucial.

With that out of the way, here are some of the more advanced day trading tricks that you can use.

1. The Ichimon Cloud

This strategy makes full use of the chart wherein 5 lines are being plotted on a price action indicator, two of them consisting of the "cloud" or top performance indicator limit for specific stocks. Another line will be the baseline which reflects the actual performance of a certain stock's price. The fourth and fifth lines would indicate the stop-loss order line that your price line must never meet if you want to profit for that day.

How this strategy works is that you open up a stock for a trade whenever the prices reach or go out of the cloud lines. You will then keep that trade open until it reaches the blue line or the day ends.

Since you are expecting a stock price to follow a trend, the third line must closely follow the trend plotted by the cloud lines. Put some considerable distance on your price and performance lines with the stop-loss order line then close if the price cloud interacts with the performance line.

The overall goal here is to make your price line follow the performance line at a close yet safe distance to protect your investments against sudden spikes in the trend.

2. The RSI/Stochastic Oscillator Strategy

This strategy will take full use of the Relative Strength Index and what is known as the Stochastic Oscillator. These indicators usually track the value of stocks and determine whether they are overbought or oversold

The premise here is to scalp the market and check for the smallest of price movements and then look for high trade activity. As such, this strategy will require multitasking and an ability to reach and adapt to sudden changes in the chart.

To use this strategy, you must first open for trade when you get signals from both the RSI and Stochastic Oscillator that certain stocks are overbought and oversold. Then, look for areas in the graph where both RSI and Oscillators meet at the lowest points, indicating a double oversold instance.

Now, if both indicators go up, that means that the stock was overbought and you should respond with a short trade. That trade should happen as often until one of the indicators go their opposite direction which should signal an opposite signal and an unfavorable price move.

For stop-loss, what you will have to remember only is that your stop-loss orders must be rather close by safe. Better yet, you should decide on a sizeable stop-loss distance and follow that trend.

3. Post-Gap with Price Action Trading

If you are the person that trades with stock-based trading assets, then this strategy might just work for you. The premise here is to set up a gap in order to properly apply the rules of this strategy. Also, you should have a list of financial assets to trade for that day as these have gaps in between the different trading periods.

This strategy begins at the start of the day which has the morning gap for the assets. Then, in between 30 minutes to an hour after opening, your financial assets will be there to be the most stable stock you have on offer.

It is important that you observe what happens in those 30 to 60 minutes after opening. If the stocks start with a strong upwards gap and then the price fills in that gap in the next hour, then there is enough reason to believe that the prices for that stock will continue to increase in that hour. But if the price continues to decrease, then maybe there is no strong growth for that stock for that session.

One other feature of this strategy is that it constantly uses price action rules to determine where and how you will exit for that session. The goal here is to end the day with a strong figure so your start of the next day will be strong as well.

For your stop-loss rule, it should be placed on the opposite side of the gap. If you open for a strong bull trade, then the stop-loss order should be at the lowest point of the gap. But if you are starting with a bear condition, then the stop-loss order should be placed at the highest point of the gap.

The Main Takeaway:

All of this talk about trends and figures only tells you that discipline is a key component for success among day traders. A mistake day traders often make is that they do not stick to their strategy, resulting in missed entry and exit points as well as massive losses by the end of the day.

Also, it takes time before you realize that you are already deviating from your strategy. As such, it might be too late to course-correct and come out strong.

Thus, it pays to write your strategy in someplace where it is easy to see and remember. Also, the apps that you will use will help you chart the performance of stocks for that day. It is up to you, then, to follow the movements of stocks closely and time your actions right.

Getting good with these strategies will take time and practice but, eventually, you'll be able to confidently open your trading day and close it with strong figures.

Timing Your Trades Correctly

Traders actually thrive by exploiting whatever conditions are present in the market that affects stock prices. In short, it is doing the most profitable action and at the right moment.

That does beg the question, though: When it is right to buy and trade stocks in the market? We're not talking about the moment that the exchanges open or close for the day. We are talking about those little windows of opportunities that you can enter in a day and start trading.

There is no exact hour for you to start trading on a single day as that depends greatly on the stock in question.However, you can look at certain aspects like:

A. Liquidity

This factor simply indicates when it is good to enter or exit a trade based on the price. What you should be looking for are "spreads" in the graph, the distance between the asking price of a stock and its bidding price. Or you could also be looking for a low slippage where the difference between the expected price of a trade and the actual price is not so wide.

What you should be looking for is a distance that is close enough but should never meet. This would tell you that you can trade stocks on that day with minimal risk of a loss.

B. Volatility

This simply indicates the expected daily price range for a certain stock. This will be the range for which any trader must operate with. The general rule is that the margin for profit or loss is greater when the volatility is high. After all, the differences in the chart will be larger if there are more figures in the range.

What you should be looking for in a manageable range of volatility. If you feel that the difference between profit and loss is quite high for that hour, maybe you should hold off on trading that stock until the gap narrows down considerably.

C. Volume

This measures frequency of activity with regards to a specific stock. To be more precise, it measures how much of that stock has been bought, sold, and traded at a given period of time. What this indicates for you is the general interest for that stock which, in turn, can tell you of an impending price jump.

More often than not, an increase in trading volume will be followed by a spike in the graph. This might be alarming for any trader but you can use that impending jump to your advantage by trading early.

Now that you know what assets to look for and how they might perform for that day, what you should be looking for is your entry point. There are tools that can help you determine this which includes:

- **The News -** There are quite a lot of market-moving news items being published by the hour. Your news source of choice should tell you when such events might happen so you could prepare accordingly.

- **ECN Quotes -** An electronic communications network will provide you with crucial information like the bidding and asking quotes from multiple market experts while also matching and executing orders for you.

What you should be looking for is a Level 2 subscription service as this provides you with access to an order book from NASDAQ. At best, this gives you an idea as to when you should buy stocks or execute orders.

When to Sell

Now that you know when to enter, the next challenge is knowing when to get out of the market before it closes for the day. Your exit strategy will be dependent on your overall strategy but common exit strategies include:

A. Fading

This strategy will involve short stocks and is best applied when the prices have been moving upwards for a while. However, such a trend should be considered only on the presumption that the stocks were either overbought, their buyers are now ready to start profiting from them, or that the buyers want to bail out ASAP.

This makes for a rather risky yet rewarding strategy as buyer activity will almost always affect stock prices for the good. At best, you can exit the market with a strong figure.

B. Scalping

One of the more popular strategies out there, scalping involves merely you selling your stocks at the moment that they start becoming profitable. It does not matter that if a better price is existing and can be achieved for that day. So as long as you are about to start making money out of that stock, you can start selling them as soon as possible.

C. The Pivot

This strategy takes advantage of a highly volatile daily market. To do this, you buy stocks at a low price at the start of the day, wait for them to rise significantly, and sell high before the market closes for the day. This strategy is rather dependent on a possible reversal of figures for stock prices. As such, the amount that you will earn at the end of the day is dependent on how much the price has risen for that day.

D. Momentum Selling

If you are the one that constantly reads the news and knows when market-changing events are about to happen, you can use this strategy. If a trend appears and is supported by a high volume of stock activity, you trade such stocks and end the day with a sizeable figure. Alternatively, you can anticipate a price surge and fade out of the market before the day ends.

Just with your entry point, you need to set up the conditions on when you want to end the day for your trading activities. Once the criteria have been set, all that is left to do is to stick to the plan.

Chapter VII: Playing the Long Game, Part I:

Understanding Risk

Regardless of how well equipped you are and how experienced you might be in trading stocks, there is never an assurance that you would profit hugely in the stock market. You can only do so much but there are just things inside the market that are beyond your control.

All of these factors can be summed up in one word: Risk

It does not matter what type of stock you invest in. Risk will always be there. As such, understanding your relationship and reward is absolutely crucial to your success as an investor/trader.

How Prevalent is Risk in Stocks?

Remember the notion that a higher risk yields higher rewards? That, technically speaking, is not correct. The more accurate statement is that a high risk yields a high potential return but the latter is less likely if the former is considerably high. That might sound confusing but that is the core premise of risk tolerance.

If you decide to invest that are riskier than the standard types in the market, there is always the chance that you will:

- **Lose your principal amount -** A poorly thought of investment at a high-yield bond runs the risk of you losing a massive portion of your funding, if not all of it.

- **Get Outpaced by Inflation -** The value of your investments is rising at a rate slower than prices. This usually happens if you invest in bonds like the ones offered by the government.

- **Lose your Retirement Money -** The money you yield from your investments is not equal to the amount that you are supposed to put up for retirement.

- **Get Overwhelmed by Fees and other Transactional Expenses -** The returns you made are barely enough to cover the expenses you have incurred in your investments.

So, how does risk come into play when it comes to your investments? Each stock type carries certain types of risk which is why it would be best that we talk about risk according to the top three common investment options.

A. Stocks

This investment option has a rather reliable return rate of 10% which is higher than what other investment options can offer. However, this also means that you have to be extra careful with them as not all companies have the same level of exposure to risk for investors.

For instance, an older and better-established company with a history of strong and consistent performance might have a high reward potential but the risk is low which makes them safe investment options. However, the same could not be said for a startup. Here, volatility is quite high which means that the chances of a high reward are rather low.

B. Bonds

A bond is one of the best ways to mitigate risk exposure in your portfolio. Since a bond is basically a reverse loan (you lending money to the company instead of the other way around), the company is obligated to pay you first as you have more to share with a creditor than your standard investor. Due to this, bonds have a generally higher rate of safety despite their lower reward rate.

And this safety is even higher if that bond in question comes from the government since they are required by law to pay you back plus interest. However, on the opposite end are the junk bonds which provide high returns but accompanied with equally high risk.

C. Mutual Funds

Since Mutual Funds are a collection of stocks and bonds, they work as a hedge that could potentially lower the risk exposure of your portfolio to a nearly negligible degree. Of course, it matters what kinds of stocks and bonds are being invested in your mutual fund. If your broker of choice decides to put your funds in bad stocks and bonds, the risk exposure not only remains but increases.

Investment-Specific Risks

Regardless of the investment type and the company offering them, you are bound to face some risks whenever you buy or trade stocks and other investment options. Here are some of the more popular risk that comes when investing in stocks.

1. Commodity Prices

This risk is inherent in companies that deal with certain commodities like gas, gold, and metals. When the prices of these commodities go up, the company benefits. But if the prices drop, then the performance of the company suffers as well as prices for their stock.

And if you think that only companies dealing with commodities can e affected by this risk, you'd be mistaken. There are some instances when companies get to suffer from price drops in a commodity especially if such a company relies on the commodity company as a supplier or as their client.

2. The News

This risk is proof of the power of media. Since they provide information that forms part of public opinion, how headlines mold the public's perception of a company will ultimately help or hinder the values of their stock.

This risk often occurs in headline-worthy events that could affect stock value such as a crash in a local economy, natural disasters occur. A company's ability to respond to such changes will matter in maintaining investor faith.

More often than not, this risk is purely "simulated" in nature. It does not have to be real or factual. So as long as the news can cause people to react en masse, the risk that a bad headline can bring to a company is rather considerable.

3. Ratings

Whenever a third-party organization assigns a certain rating to a company, such a rating will also affect how investors would perceive the company. For example, the analysis rating that a company gets in the stock market will cause swings in public perception and the company will have to do damage control just to prevent losses. Again, this is like the news but with more number crunching.

4. Obsolescence

The fact that the very nature of a company or its products and services is going to be out-phased can deal a serious blow on its stock value. This is a problem that long-running companies often deal with as they have to keep up with the pace of technology.

One common example of this is when a younger company enters into the market, offering a product that is similar to what older companies offer but is better and cheaper. This risk is expected to increase as the years pass with more technologies being created and the knowledge gap of consumers getting narrower and narrower.

5. **Public Scandals**

Let us say that an auditor performs an analysis on the company and discovers that there are discrepancies in its financial statements. Worse, let us say that the leadership of that company is involved in embezzlement schemes, are not paying their taxes honestly, and other news-worthy scandals.

If such were to ever happen, the damage to a company's standing among its investors will be severely damaged. This is what happened to Enron when the company was involved in a series of high-publicized schemes as well as a massive environmental calamity. As soon as investors are made aware that company leadership is unethical, their most natural response would be to bail out. This causes a massive drop in stock value as well as a near-irreparable reputation.

Systemic Risks

We've only talked so far about the risks that you encounter when investing in stocks. However, the risk is so prevalent that it is even inherent to the market itself. In other words, there are factors out there that are absolutely out of your control and yet would throw a proverbial wrench in all of your plans.

If you listen closely to the stock market news, you'll come across certain news items about seemingly unrelated events that investors fear would affect prices in the stock market. Seriously, how does a person getting elected as the US President or the British Prime Minister have to do with prices for stocks? What does a worldwide pandemic have to do with the stock market?

The truth is that, regardless of the explanation, the occurrence of such events would generally influence activity in various stock markets. To understand how you need to know in what forms these risks would take.

A. Politics

This risk comes from changes in administration, governmental policies, shifts in political movements and ideologies, and other events that could impact the movement of commodities across the world.

For instance, the war in the Middle East caused massive changes in the stock market in the 90s to 2000s while the UK stock market experienced a period of volatility when the country decided to leave the European Union. Another good example is the political turmoil in Venezuela in the 2000s which obliterated its stock market.

B. National Debt

This risk usually happens when a state cannot honor the debts it has incurred at the World Bank or the International Monetary Fund. Due to the debt, all financial products like stocks, bonds, and mutual funds are the ones that are the first to get hit. This happened in Greece in 2009 when the country was unable to pay off its debt and, as a consequence, stock prices in the Greek economy plummeted.

C. The Environment

These events are either unforeseen or, if foreseen, unavoidable. A single natural disaster can do quite a lot of damage in the stock market, especially in a major financial center.

D. Market Value

Due to prevailing trends, the value of investments will eventually fluctuate. However, in some cases, they will lose quite a lot of value which leads to a crash.

Recessions are perhaps one of the most direct threats to your portfolio's value. When the US real estate market collapsed in 2008, the value of investments in the US Stock Market declined as well. Of course, this sparked a frenzy in investors scrambling to bail out before they lose all their money.

E. Interest Rates

A change in interest rates at the market is known to slow an entire economy down. The reason for this is that companies and investors are now a bit more cautious with their spending activities. This primarily affects bonds but stocks can also be affected by changes in interest rates.

How to Tell If You are in a Bull or Bear Market

How could you ever possibly know what you are in a bull market or a bear market. So far, we have been talking about taking advantage of whatever conditions are in the market but how does an investor prepare themselves for an upcoming change of trends in the stock market?

First things first, there is no proper definition of a bull or bear market. Nobody can tell you exactly what these market conditions are. You can only tell that the market is entering the bull or bear phase by paying attention to changes in stock trends or figures.

A. Bull Market

The bull market is where the market follows an upswing phase. You can tell that things are going well when performance indexes grow by 20%. however, that growth is not enough. It should immediately follow a decline of 20% or more.

So, if the market's drop is at 25% but this has risen to 19%, then the market is entering its bull phase. The market will remain in that phase so as long as the index does not go back to 20% and above range.

If you want to be a bit fancier, you can also declare a bull phase if the rise and drop occur at the closing of a market. As such, if the market closes at the 20% limit, then you as an investor are exiting it at a bull phase.

B. Bear Market

If the bull market is an upwards swing, then the bear market is the complete opposite. When the index drops to 20% following a gain of 20% or more, then the market is entering its bear phase.

Also, unlike bull markets which follow one after another, bear markets only follow after a bull market. There is no bear market after a bear market. So as long as the index remains at the 20% drop, then it is a singular bear phase no matter how many times the market has closed for the day.

The Bottomline

The prevalent presence of risk in the market will tell you that there is no such thing as a risk-free stock market. Also, there is no right or wrong response to risk. Whenever a potential risk pops up, there is the option to hold on to your investments until things get better or bail out and take whatever portion of your money remains.

That being said, there is a way for you to mitigate the risks that you encounter without necessarily deviating from your plans.

Chapter VIII: Playing the Long Game, Part II: Mitigating Risk

Now that you know that risk can come from anywhere in the stock market, the next thing that you'll have to do is to reduce its effects on your investment portfolio. There are multiple ways to mitigate risks in the stock market and they could be used by you regardless of your overall strategy.

But, before we go to those, it is best that we settle something else first.

Managing Debts

Your capital is your most important asset like a stock investor bar your skills and tools. After all, you cannot invest without money. However, just remember that brokerages like the S&P 500 get a 10% return as an average every year. Although that is a rather healthy return for any investment, that is still considerably lower than any interest rate that a credit card could impose on you which could go as high as 15%.

As such, if you have credit obligations, it is best that you clear them first before you start or resume investing in the stock market. The same also goes for personal loans.

But, in some instances, credit card debt is unavoidable. So, when should you start prioritizing your credit card and personal debt before investing? There is no exact figure but, just to be safe, hold off on investing when you have a credit card or loan with an interest rate over 5%.

If you are serious about investing in the stock market regardless if you have debt or not, then it is recommended that you set aside money specifically for investing. An emergency fund should be some savings of sorts by you where you have set aside a portion of your monthly earnings in preparation for investing.

This means that you should have already prepared years in advance before you start venturing into the stock market. If that is not possible, then make sure all of your debts are clear before you start investing.

At least, this way, you don't have to juggle two different obligations at the same time.

Dollar-Cost Averaging: Advantages and Disadvantages

A few chapters ago, we talked about how dollar-cost averaging is used. But what benefits does it offer? The most direct one would be that it spreads your risk exposure evenly over time.

The other advantage is automation. With a set price every month, you won't have to spend a lot of time mulling over how much you are going to spend every month and how many shares you should acquire. There are even apps that allow you to automate not only the allocation of budget but also the actual investing in stocks,

Another advantage is that it removes the need on finding the right entry and exit point every time the market opens. At the very least, you can do your activities without having to wait for a good market swing.

But if there was ever a disadvantage with dollar-cost averaging, it would be that it is not enough to deal with the cost of long-term averaging. The strategy is good only for returns that are below the average.

AI-based Index Funding

As of now, you should realize that actively managing your funds is rather expensive. After all, you are paying someone to do all the investing for you   so you could beat the average market returns. In the long run, this is going to consume a huge portion of your money.

Of course, you cannot remove the element of error since another person is running the operation on your behalf. As a result, a lot of actively managed funds underperform in the market.

As such, it would be better if you opt for a passive index funding platform. Their system works by the use of an AI that can accurately mimic the movement of indexes like the S&P 500. Since this is an AI, there is no need to pay for a fund manager, and human error is likewise removed.

What you will be paying for instead are the expense ratios which are lower in cost than the salary of a fund manager by 90%. In other words, you can protect keep more of your money by letting an automated computer system do your funding activities for you.

Surprises in Earnings

Picture this scenario: have you ever closely monitored the earnings of a certain company, expecting them to follow a certain path, only to deviate in one key point? For instance, you were expecting the earnings for one company to plummet further only for them to rise significantly in just one day.

It's a welcome surprise, right? After all, the earnings have actually beaten the predictions of industry experts. Technically, you should be worried. Surprises are a major indication that forecasts for that day were not as accurate as you want them to be.

If the stocks that you have invested in are known to earn in large amounts and the analysts' forecasts are way off, then the risk is greater for you. This level of uncertainty can make you feel apprehensive in speculating where a company's performance will take them in the future.

Think about it: if a lot of people were wrong in their earnings forecast for that one company, where else did they screw up in that day?

So, how could you tell that there will be surprises in a company's earnings? Here are some aspects to look for.

- **Limited to No Coverage -** Not a lot of analysts are monitoring that stock.
- **The Company is New -** New companies have not a lot of history to indicate good performance. Thus investors and analysts do not have much to go about in predicting their earnings.
- **No Consistent Trend -** When analysts do cover that stock, their estimates, and predictions do not share any common point

or trend. This only reflects the fact that there is a lot of uncertainty regarding that company.

Naturally, predictions for a company become stabler the longer they perform in the company. Whether good or bad, a history and a sizeable performance index can help analysts predict what might just happen next, with key emphasis on the word "might".

Low P/E

A lot of investors have this thinking that bargain-level trading is the best way to succeed in the stock market. And to find such cheap bargains, these investors use the Price to Earnings ratio.

If the stock is earning a level of profit higher than its price, the P/E ratio would classify this stock as undervalued. This means that they can buy the stock cheap and then sell it at a higher price later on.

However, looks can be deceiving. The P/E ratio might be low but it does not account for the wider range of risks that could ultimately affect stock prices in the future. The point is that you should never be completely dependent on P/E to determine which stocks are cheap.

As a matter of fact, you are better off using other ratios like the Cash Flow Per Share ratio and even the analysis of industry experts.

Diversifying Your Portfolio

Perhaps one of the most potent strategies you can use in mitigating risk is to diversify your portfolio. The act of diversification simply pertains to adding different types of investments to your portfolio. The concept here is that a higher variety of diversification in your portfolio will yield a high return while lowering risk by spreading your presence in different sectors of the stock market.

Diversifying your investments is not exactly a new idea. It really takes care and attention to detail in order to diversify your investments instead of being reactionary and impulsive. In essence, you diversifying your investments should have been part of your plan and not just you responding to any exposure to risk.

With that out of the way, here are some tips to remember in order to diversify your investments.

1. **Vary Stocks**

Your individual stocks should not be identical to one another as this is a surefire way o losing value in case the worst were to happen. For instance, you should not invest in one type of stock for $100.00 per share every time you enter the market. Try to look for cheaper stocks that allow you to buy more on the same budget.

Also, there is nothing that says that you cannot invest in the competition. Each company stock has its own rate of return, growth, and other performance metrics. The same goes for bonds as you want varying levels of credit features, term duration, and maturity periods.

The less homogenized your stock is at a glance, the more secure it will be as time passes.

2. **Mind the Quality**

Having a lot of investments does not make for a diversified portfolio on its own. What you should be focusing on is the variety of such investments which means your portfolio should not be focused on stocks, bonds, funds, commodities, and other options on their own.

To truly make your portfolio diverse in quality, you need to understand what each investment type brings to it. A diversified portfolio will have:

- Stocks for growth
- Bonds for an income boost
- Real estate funds as a safety net against inflation
- Global investments for further growth and buying power
- Cash for stability

3. Diversify by Investment Categories

You can take diversification even further by investing in different stocks within the same category. For instance, if you are started with some healthcare companies, perhaps you can look into stocks offered by financial companies, food services, and retail. At the very least, this prevents your portfolio from losing value if one sector faces a serious crisis for a period of time.

If you do not have a lot of capital, diversifying your portfolio by buying individual shares might become expensive. As such, your next best option is through mutual funds. As was discussed extensively a few chapters ago, mutual funds are like a collection of investment types coming from different sectors at a fraction of the cost.

To truly take advantage of mutual funds, look for types that feature investment options at a global scale or coming from different seemingly unrelated markets. They should instantly protect and diversify your portfolio.

4. Spread Out

Sticking to the stocks or sectors that you are most comfortable with might be good but it's best that you don't get stuck in those areas for too long. You can quickly spread out with the help of a mutual fund where you can choose to invest in other companies. These companies do not even have to be new ones. They can be the companies whose products you use every day or, at the very least, are ran by people that you know.

Of course, stocks are not the only thing to consider when you are an investor. The different investment options provided in Chapter II have their own set of advantages and potential reward yields which you can use to create a safety net for your investments. As of now, commodities like gold offer the highest rate of security as they are known to perform reliably even under bad economic conditions.

Also, don't just invest in your local market. Think about going national or global as there are a lot of other companies out there who are looking for overseas investors and whose local markets have a more lenient margin of competition that you can take part in.

However, do take care that you do not spread yourself too thinly. You should keep your portfolio at a certain manageable size. At least, add 20 or 30 new stocks to your portfolio for a year to diversify it.

5. Finding a Good Balance Between Stocks and Bonds

You could take things a step further by adding more individualized stocks and bonds to your portfolio. The ratio of stocks compared to bonds in your portfolio will depend greatly on your tolerance and overall investment strategy but make sure that the bonds do not overwhelm your stocks.

If, for example, you have 30 shares acquired this year, you can add somewhere in between 5 to 10 bonds into your portfolio. Experts even recommend that you stick to an 8:2 or 9:1 distribution between your stocks and bonds.

The reason for this is that stocks and bonds actually behave differently in the market. Bonds already have a high rate of security but they do not have a high yield. On the other hand, stocks have a high yield but a low rate of security. You can use the bonds to make your portfolio more secure while stocks are there to increase the flow of cash.

6. Mind the Risk Exposure

One way to mitigate risk is to pick stocks with different rates of return. This is to make sure that you can still enjoy fro substantial gains in case on company or sector under-performs for a period of time.

This is where going global can also help you as some countries have stock exchanges with different dynamics, competition, and risk exposure which should balance out the inherent disadvantages of your local stock market.

However, while diversification protects you from losses, it leaves you open to another risk: the amount you pay in annual returns. This is because anything that increases or lowers risk will also increase or lower the potential for rewards.

7. Know When to Make an Exit

One mistake that a lot who use dollar-cost averaging and automated funds as strategies make is that they do not bother to pay attention to what is going on. Those systems and fund managers can only do so much but an investor still has to make judgment calls here and there to optimize their investments.

Keep in touch with the market and pay attention to any potential change. You should also be aware of whatever changes are being made in the companies you invest in. This will help you make informed decisions and determine when it is time to start cutting on your losses.

The Basics of Hedging

Since risk is unavoidable, the last counter you could use some form of loss protection. This is where hedging comes into play and it simply involves an investor setting up fail-safes to protect themselves from the negative impacts of an unwanted event.

The best way to understand Hedging is to think of it as insurance. Whenever something happens to the assets being covered which, in this instance, are your investments, something will protect you from the losses you might potentially incur.

Funnily enough, some Hedging measures act like actual insurance. For example, let us say that you own shares at Company 456 which operates in the foodservice industry. Although the company has a long-standing history of good performance and profit, you are worried about its short-term performance due to a massive downturn in the industry.

To protect yourself in case of losses in Company 456, you buy a put option where you are given the right to sell your shares in the market at a fixed price. Now, if stock prices were to fall way below the put option price, the losses you incurred will be offset by gains in the same put option.

Hedging also works in instances of a company relying on certain commodities. Let us say that Company 963 produces beer and is thus reliant on the prices of yeast in the market. As such, 963 would find themselves in a bind should prices for yeast increase tremendously.

To protect against such an event, 963 might enter into either a future or forward contract which allows the company to buy yeast at a set price for a period of time in case of the aforementioned price increase.

These are just some of the so-called hedges that can be put up by investors and companies in the preparation of unwanted events. However, you yourself can put up a hedging system for your investments using some of the strategies below.

A. **Don't Forget About Cash**

Savings accounts, cash deposits, and certificates of deposit are partially unaffected by market volatility. The reason for this is that cash posses agility and versatility that allows it to thrive where other investments can get hampered. Of course, this comes at a price as cash has little to no returns and does not provide a lot of buying power in case of inflation.

B. Invest in Gold

Gold has perhaps one of the most dependable track records out of all commodities. Even though prices would fluctuate, it's performance has never dipped below the negative for over a century now. Having some gold investments should at least provide some stability to your investment in case of a massive economic downturn.

C. **Do Covered Calls**

A covered call involves you selling out money call options against long equity positions. Although it does not reduce your exposure to risk whatsoever, it at least offset the potential losses you might suffer. Just remember that this strategy works well only with individual stocks that are set to drop in prices. Should the stock price rise above the strike price, the losses you might incur at the option position will offset whatever gains you were to receive on equity.

D. **Inverse Returns**

As of now, you can buy ETFs and other financial securities that seem to appreciate their price when other stocks are losing money. Just keep in mind that most of these products are leveraged which will require capital in order to be hedged. However, they can also be traded through an ordinary stock trading account.

D. **Go On the Defense**

Investing in defensive sectors like utilities, consumer products, and even bonds is not exactly a purely hedging maneuver. It's a mix between hedging and diversification, in fact. But what makes this strategy work is that it shifts the focus of your portfolio towards low beta assets.

What that simply means is that your investment's exposure remains the same (which keeps the potential reward at the same level, too) but gives enough leeway for you to keep yourself active even under unfavorable market conditions.

To Conclude

Even as you attempt to apply these risk mitigation strategies, you have to remember that they are just as effective as how you applied them. If you do not time your strategy right like in options or futures, you might end up spending more where others are dealing with cheaper prices.

Also, none of these strategies would ultimately remove risk. There is still that off-chance that, even with all your fail-safes, you would still end up losing at the closing of a day. However, they do at least minimize the effects so you only end up losing some of the value of your stocks, not all of it.

Conclusion

At the end of the day, after everything that you have learned, there is still one question to ask:

What does success look like for an investor like me?

That might sound like a loaded question because, in reality, it is. Every stock investor has their own way of answering this question. But, as a way of summarizing all that you have learned in this book, success does take a certain form for every stock market investor out there.

First, and the most basic of all, would be an investing lifestyle that is grounded on the basics and discipline. In all honesty, you must never treat the whole investing/trading activity like gambling. This activity is not about pure luck (although that does factor in some way) but a careful study of what's going on in the market.

Also, it involves fighting off the more negative tendencies that you might develop as an investor. This includes becoming impulsive with your decisions or abandoning your plans at the first mention of trouble. More often than not, it is the disciplined traders and investors that last long in the market.

The second would be an intelligent usage of all the tools, skills, and strategies at your disposal.

Every trader/investor has their own unique experience in the market even if they trade the same stocks and use the same analysis tools. You have to remember that there is a high degree of uncertainty within the market despite all those forecasts and speculations.

As such, you should strive to apply what you have learned in a way that fits your situation, not the other way around. A good investor not only knows what analysis tool to use or ratio to look into but can also adapt to sudden changes in the market. Your adaptability and creativity as a stock investor will matter more than your ability to quote complex analysis formulas.

Lastly, and perhaps the most important of all, is that feeling that you have a greater degree of understanding about the variables in the stock market. There is actually no way to "beat the system". Regardless of how much you earn at the end of the day, the stock market gets to function the same way as it did ever since the 1920s. Regardless of which companies and traders won big that day and what conditions there are in the market currently, the stock market will open again the next day to do the same thing. And the day after that.

As such, what you can only hope to achieve here is to end the trading day on your terms. This means finding the right stocks to trade and open, trading the same at a price most valuable to you, and exiting the market with way more value or money than you started just a few hours ago. And once all of this done, you can get to open with strong figures in the next day.

That might not inspire a lot of confidence but that is true if your sole parameter of success is earning a lot as a stock investor. As was stated in the beginning, what shall determine victory for any stock investor is not profit but survivability. If you can get to do what you want to d in the stock market every day without bleeding your funds dry, then you can consider yourself a successful stock investor.

And with that comes the end of this book. I hope you have learned a lot regarding the basics of investing and moving around the stock market. All that is left to do now is to apply all that you have learned and achieve whatever degree of success you have set for yourself.

Good luck!

Bibliography

Books

- Graham, B., Zweig, B., and Buffett, W.E.,"The Intelligent Investor: The Definitive Book on Value Investing"., 2006
- Mladjenovic, P., "Stock Investing for Dummies", 2020
- Aziz, A., "How to Day Trade for a Living: A Beginner's Guide to Trading Tools and Tactics, Money Management, Discipline and Trading Psychology", 2016
- Malkiel, B., "A Random Walk Down Wall Street: The Time-Tested Strategy to Be Successful", 2020
- Snow, T., "Investing QuickStart Guide: The Simplified Beginner's Guide to Successfully Navigating the Stock Market, Growing Your Wealth & Creating a Secure Financial Future:, 2018
- Bogle, J., "The Little Book of Common Sense Investing: The Only Way to Guarantee Your Fair Share of Stock Market Returns", 2017

Journals

- Peavy, J.W., and Safran, J., "How Efficiently Does the Stock Market Process News of Price Anomalies?', The Journal of Investing, 2010
- Foster, J.D., Reidy, D., Misra, T., Joshua, S., "Narcissism and Stock Market Investing:

Correlates and Consequences of Cocksure Investing", Personality and Individual Differences, 2011
- Clark, E.A, and Tunaru, R.,"Emerging Markets: Stock Market Investing with Political Risk", SSRN Electronic Journal, 2001

Website Articles

- Chen, J., "Risk", Investopedia, October 6, 2020. Link: https://www.investopedia.com/terms/r/risk.asp
- Kay, M.F., "3 Reasons Why Investors Fail and What We Can Do About It", Forbes.com, October 29, 2013. Link: https://www.forbes.com/sites/michaelkay/2013/10/29/3-reasons-why-investors-fail-and-what-we-can-do-about-it/?sh=71624871a17b
- Beers, B., "Hedging vs. Speculation: What's the Difference?, Investopedia, May 4, 2019. Link: https://www.investopedia.com/ask/answers/difference-between-hedging-and-speculation

www.ingramcontent.com/pod-product-compliance
Lightning Source LLC
Chambersburg PA
CBHW071417210326
41597CB00020B/3548